CABIN LIFE

PHOTO JOURNAL

ROBERT ORNIG

"BUILDING AN OFF THE GRID HOME IS ONE OF THE HARDEST, BUT ALSO ONE OF THE MOST REWARDING THINGS YOU WILL EVER DO."

GARY COLLINS,

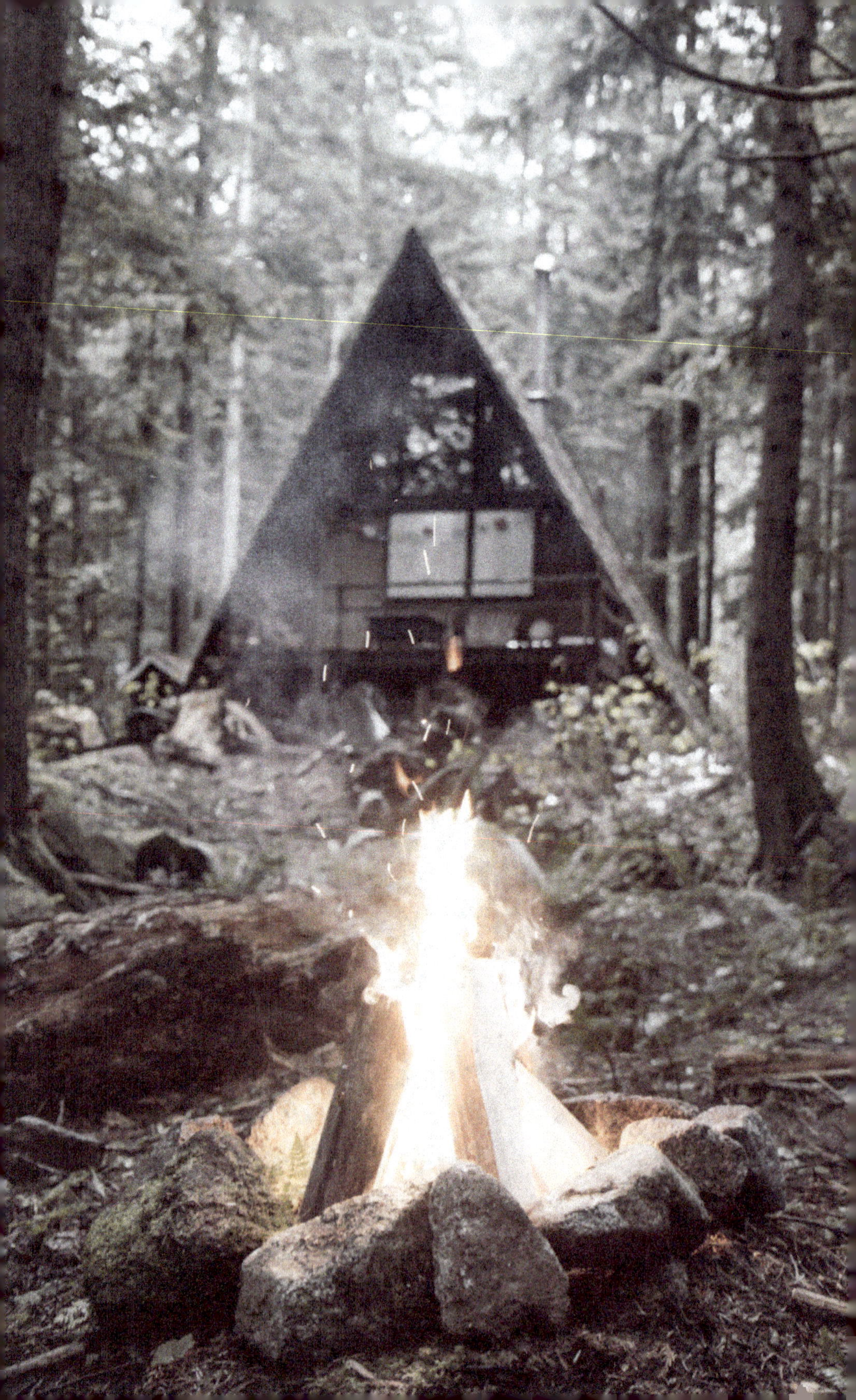

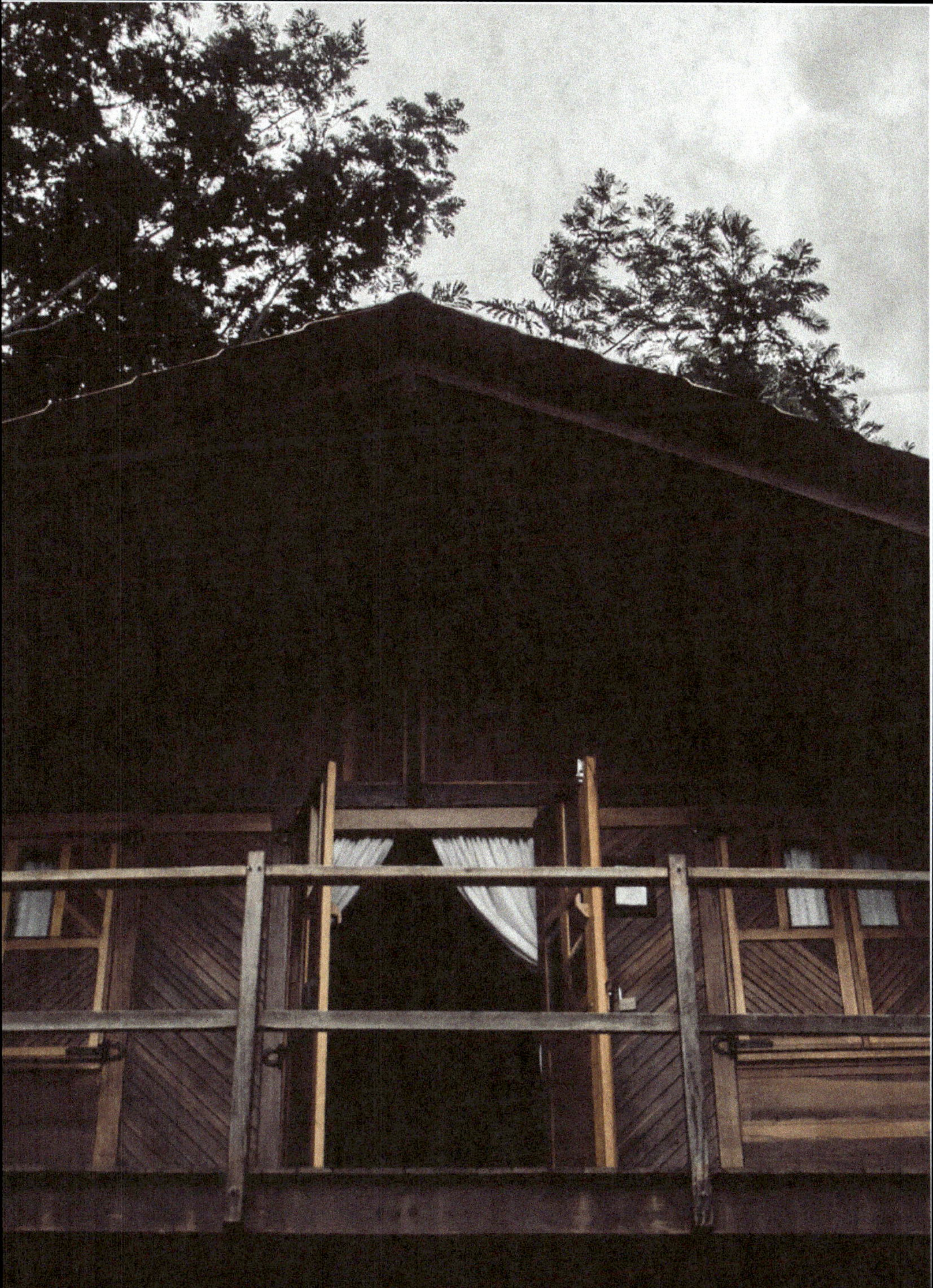

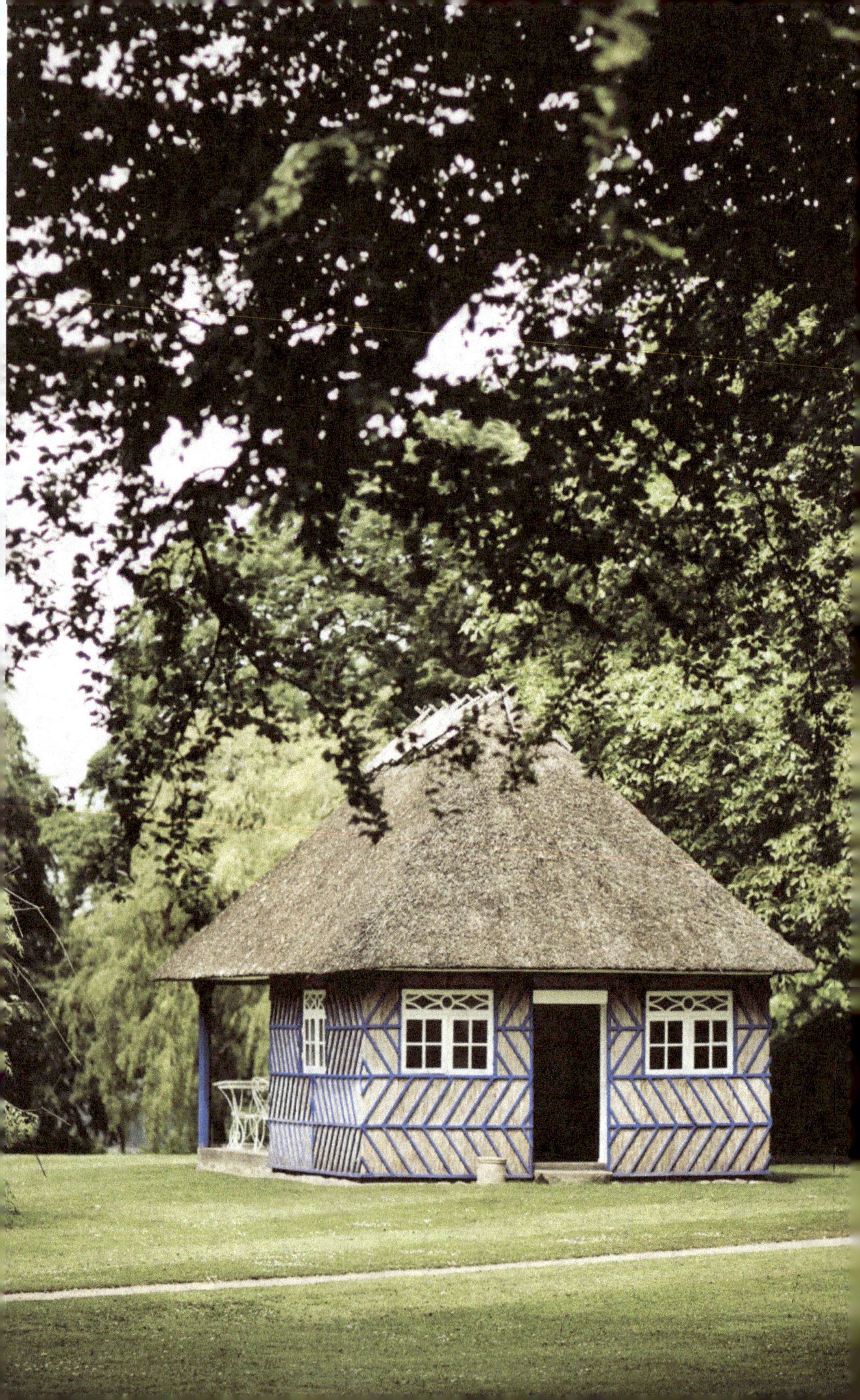

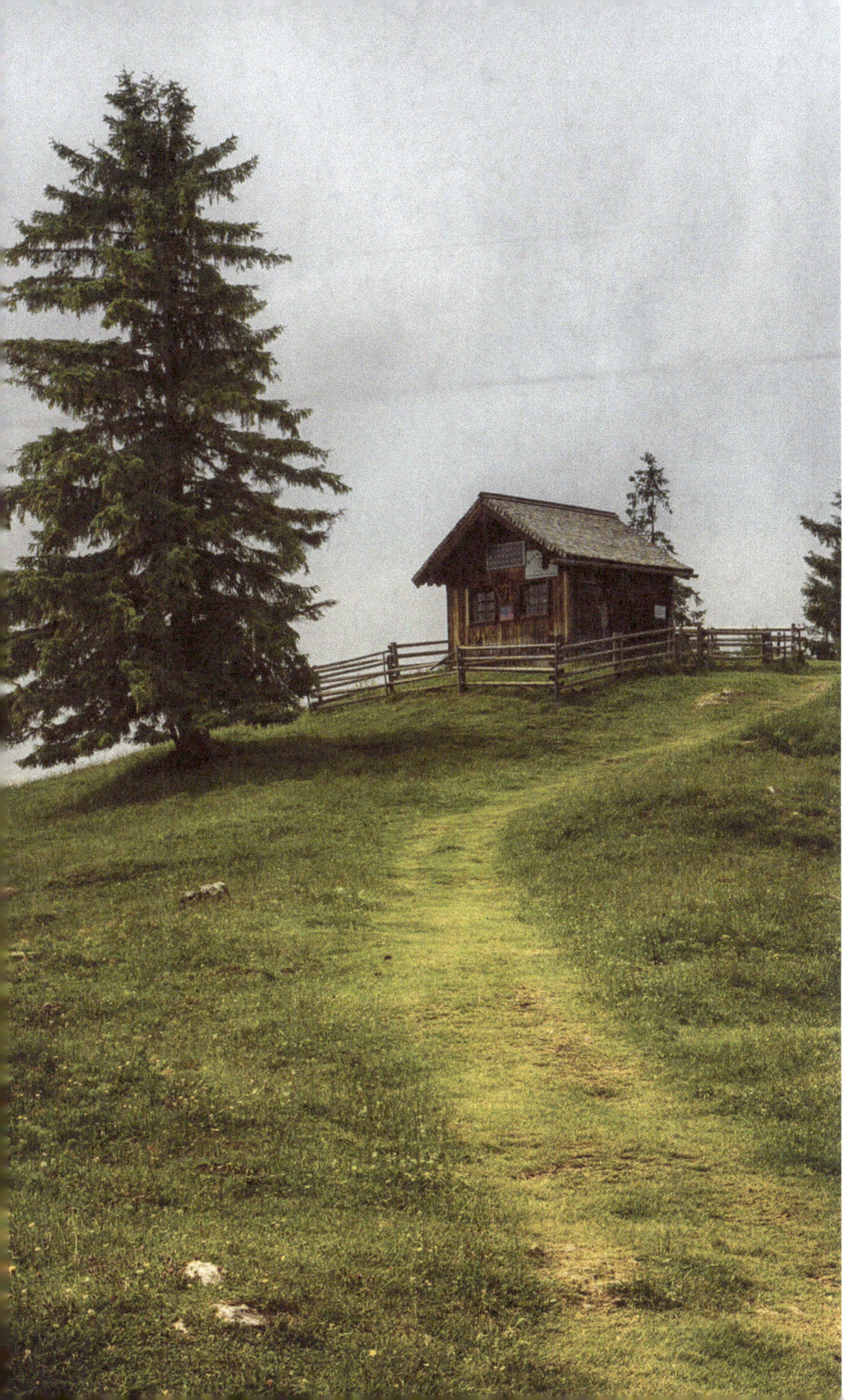

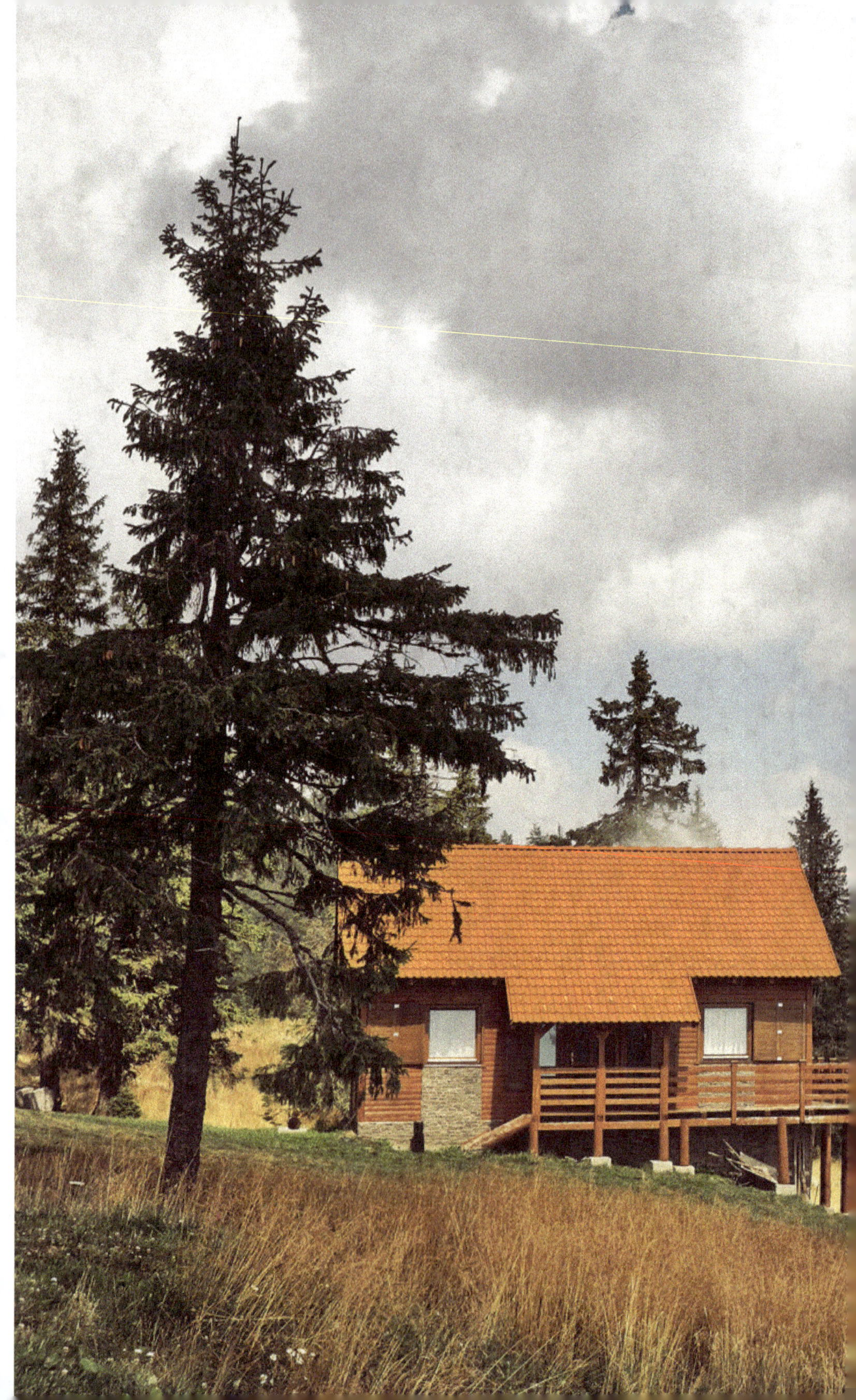

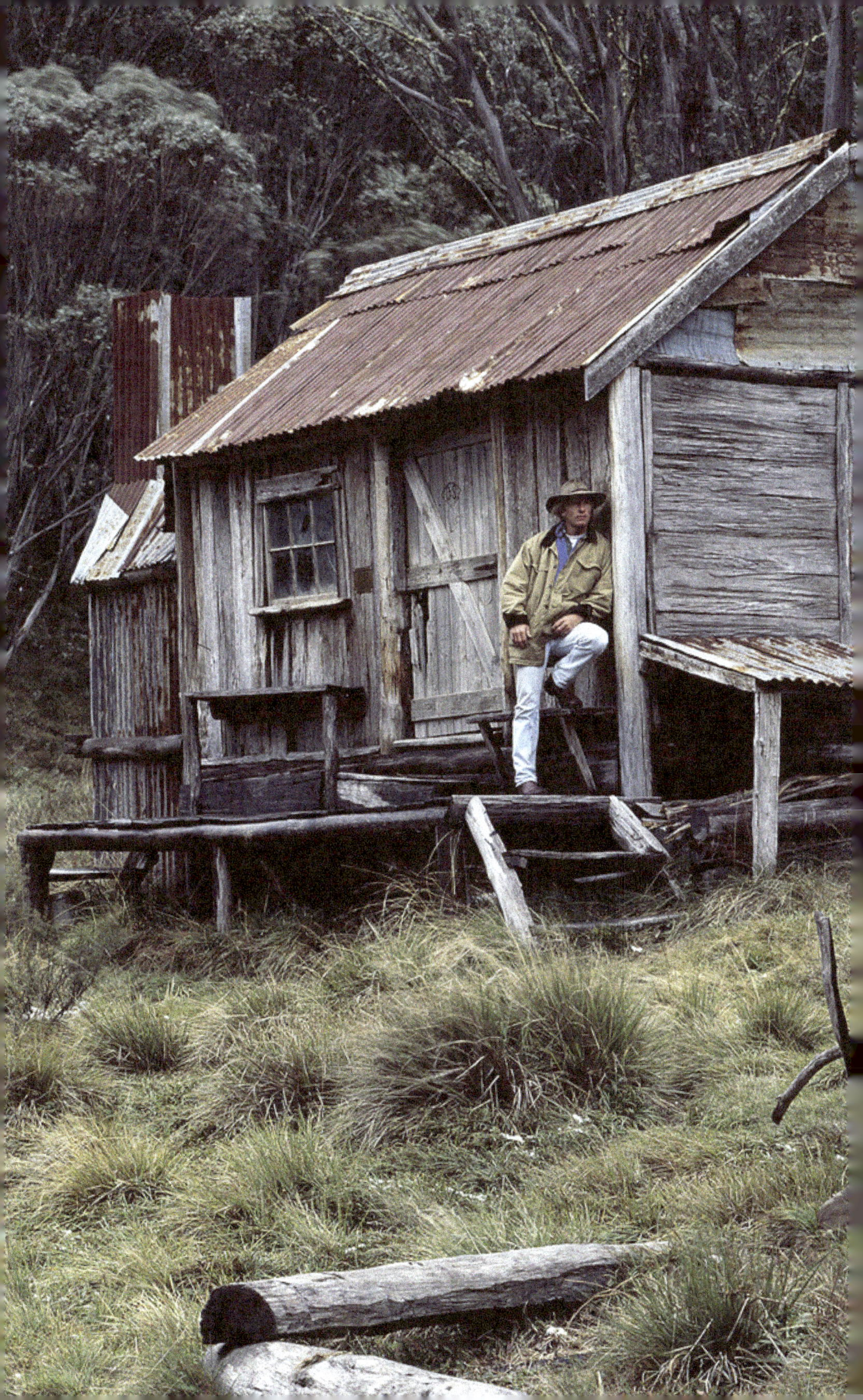

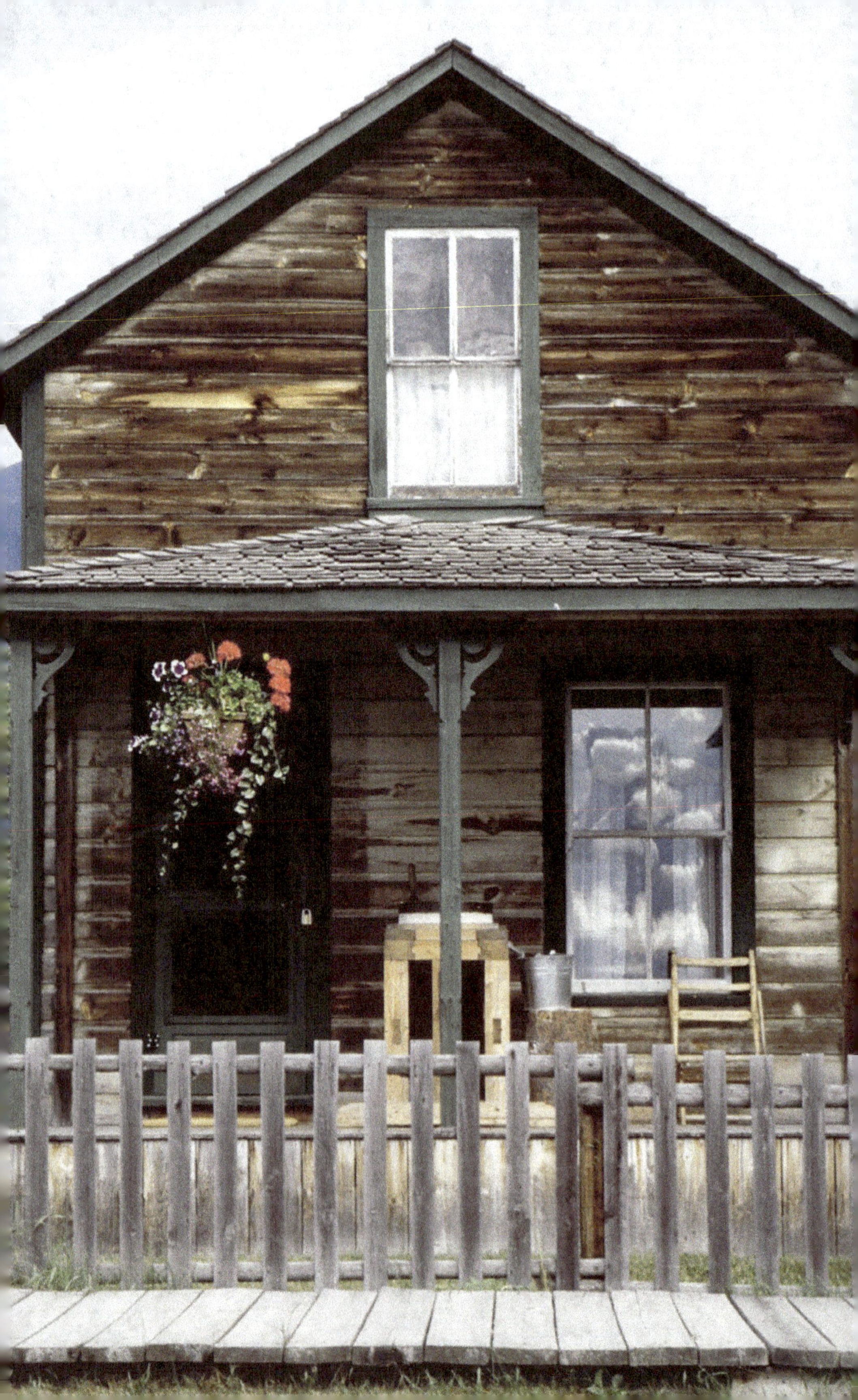

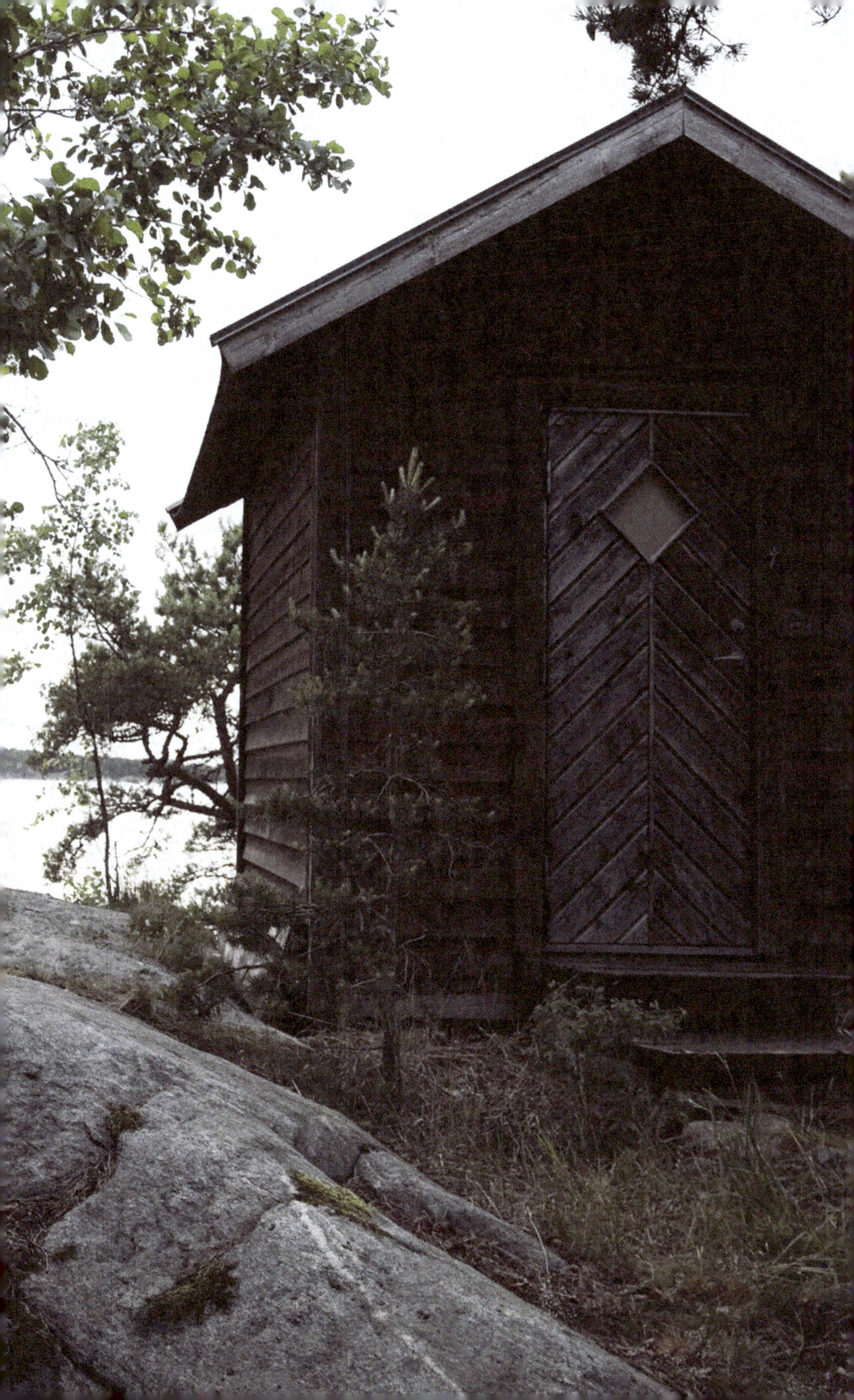

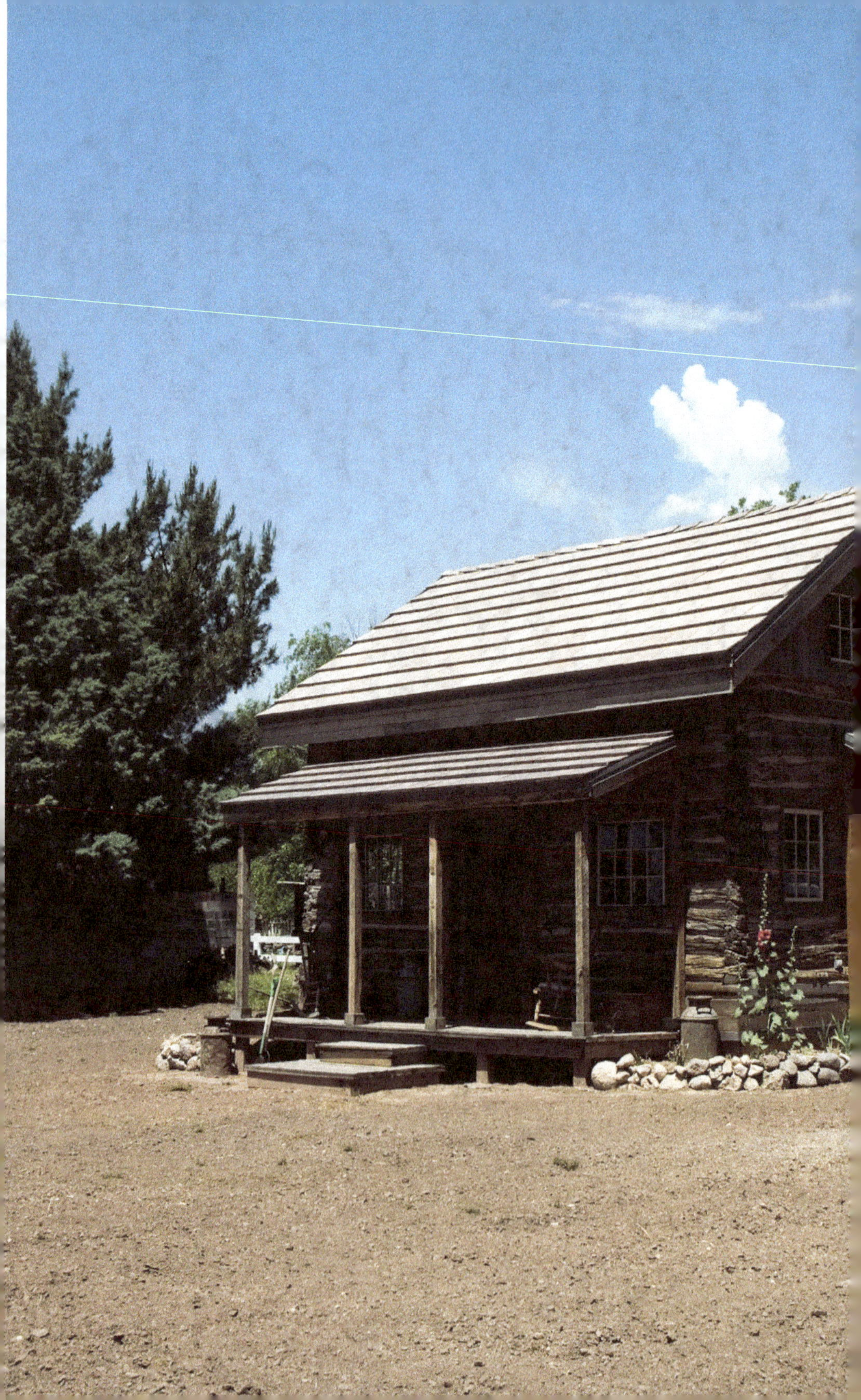

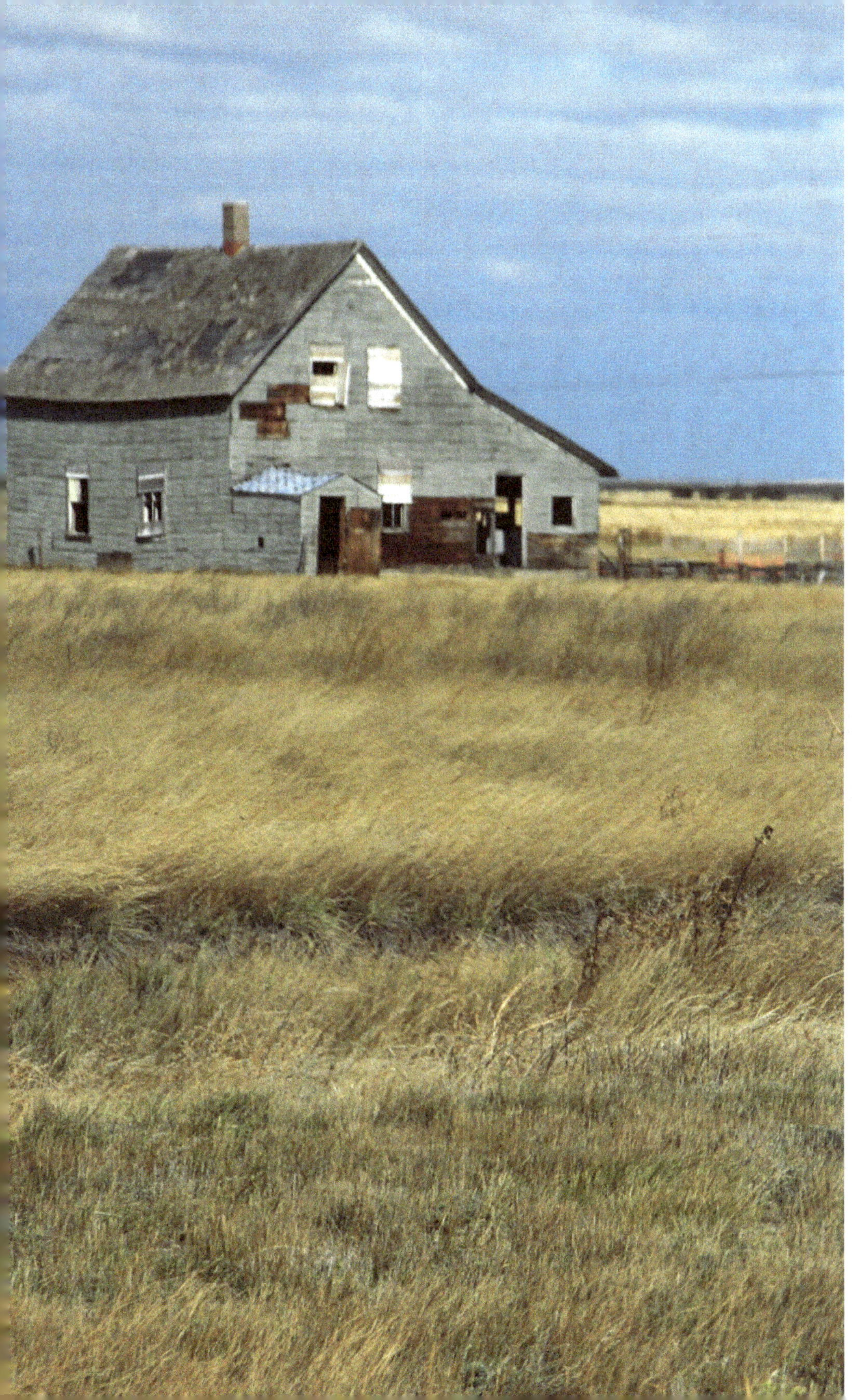

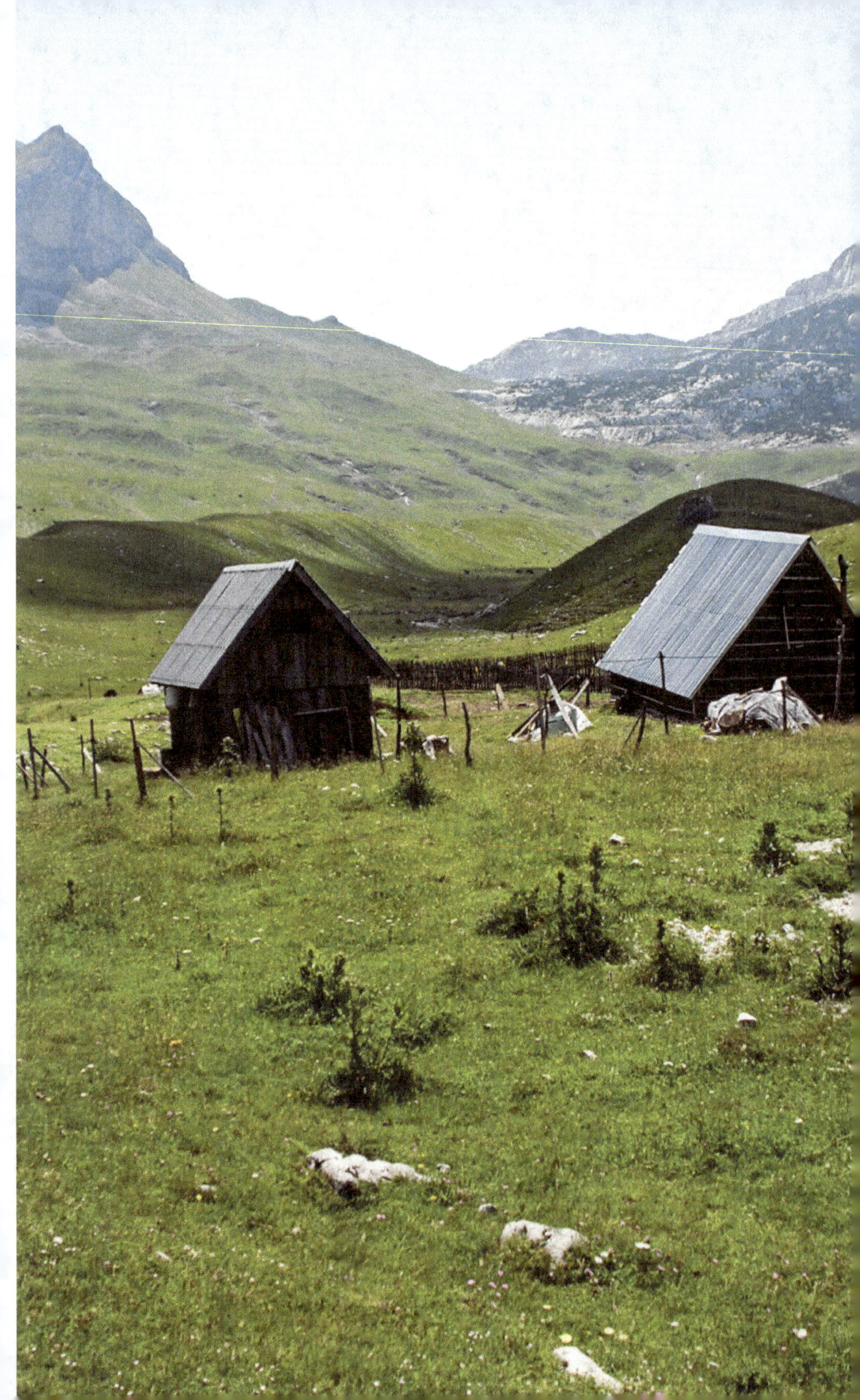

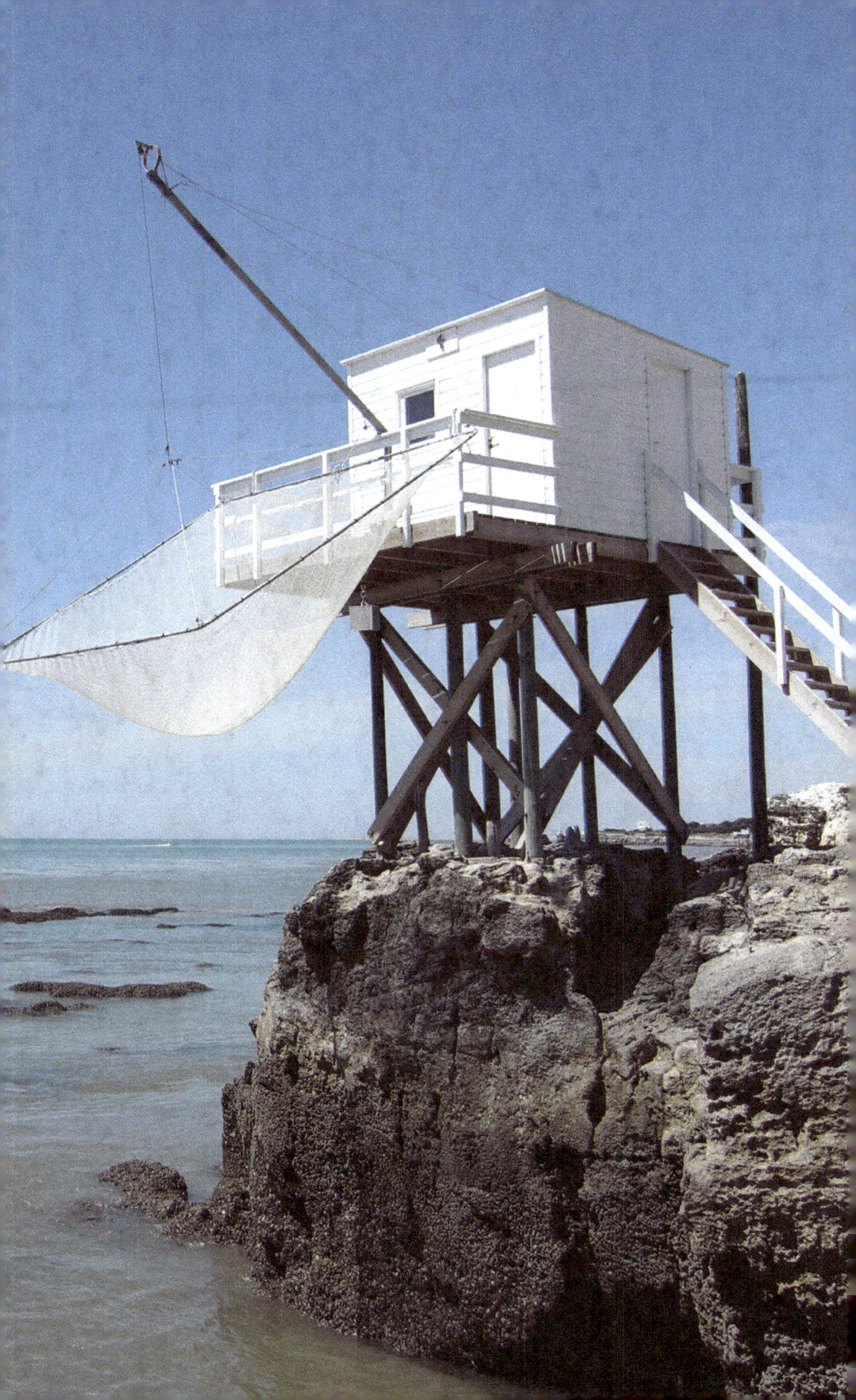

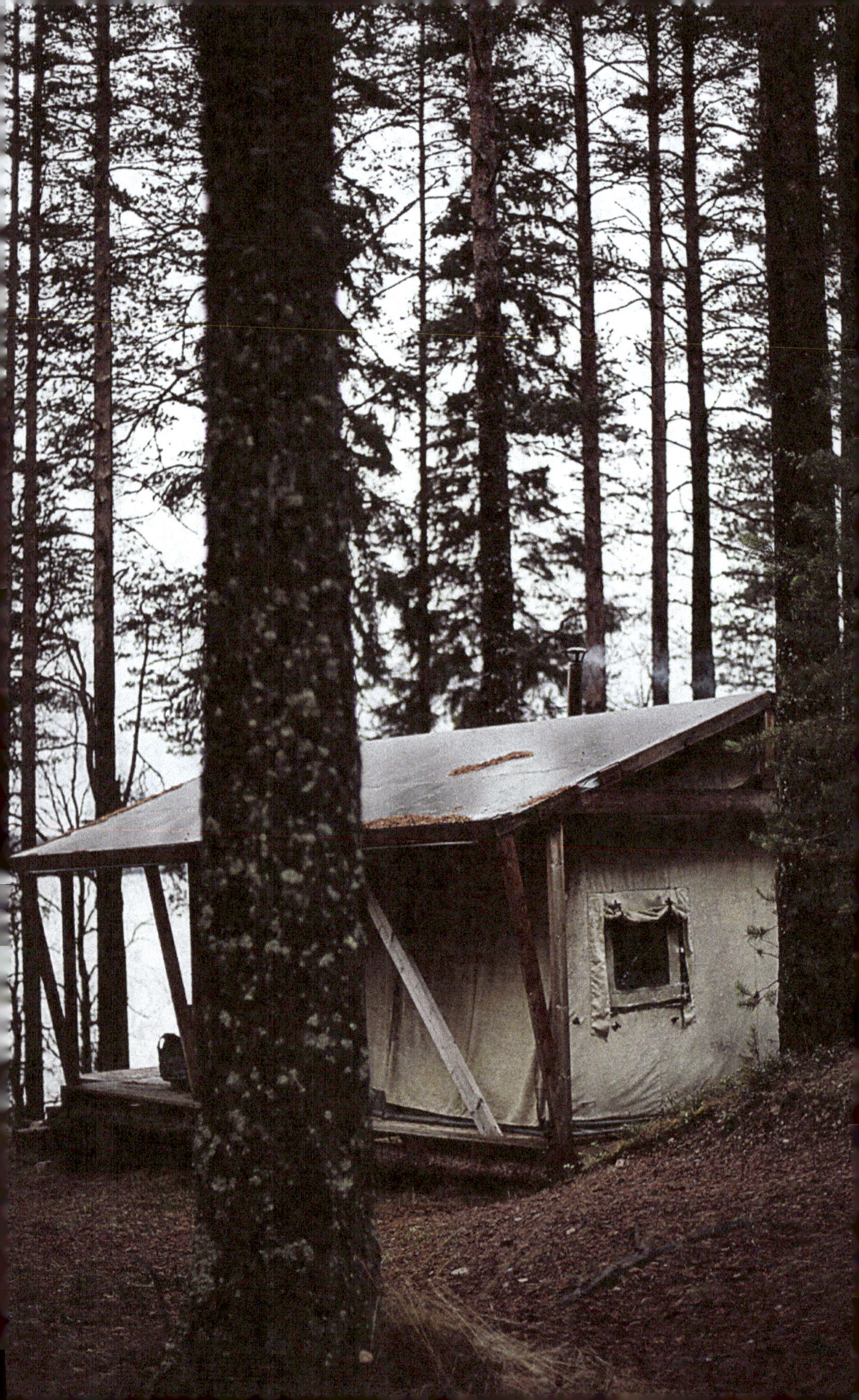

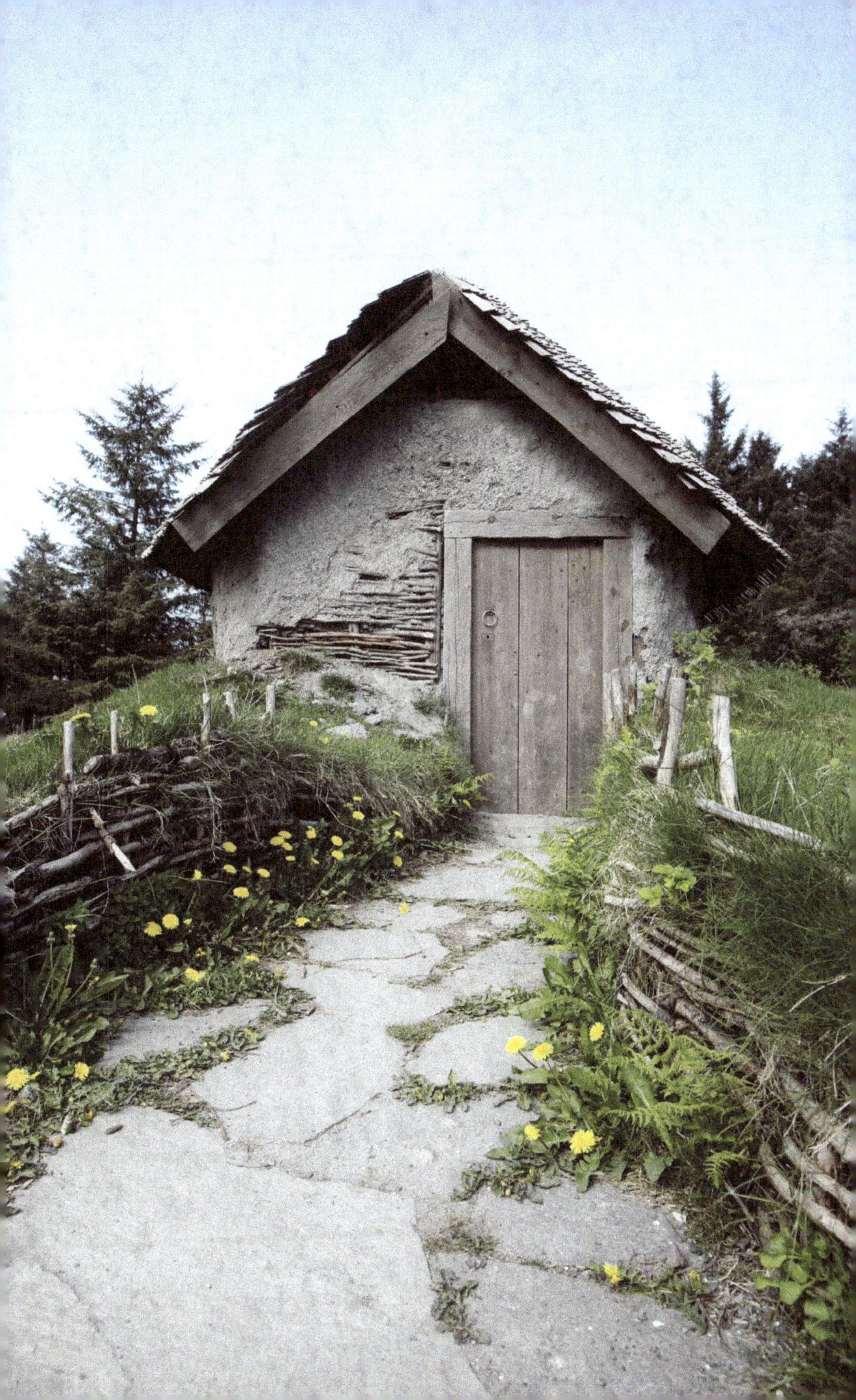

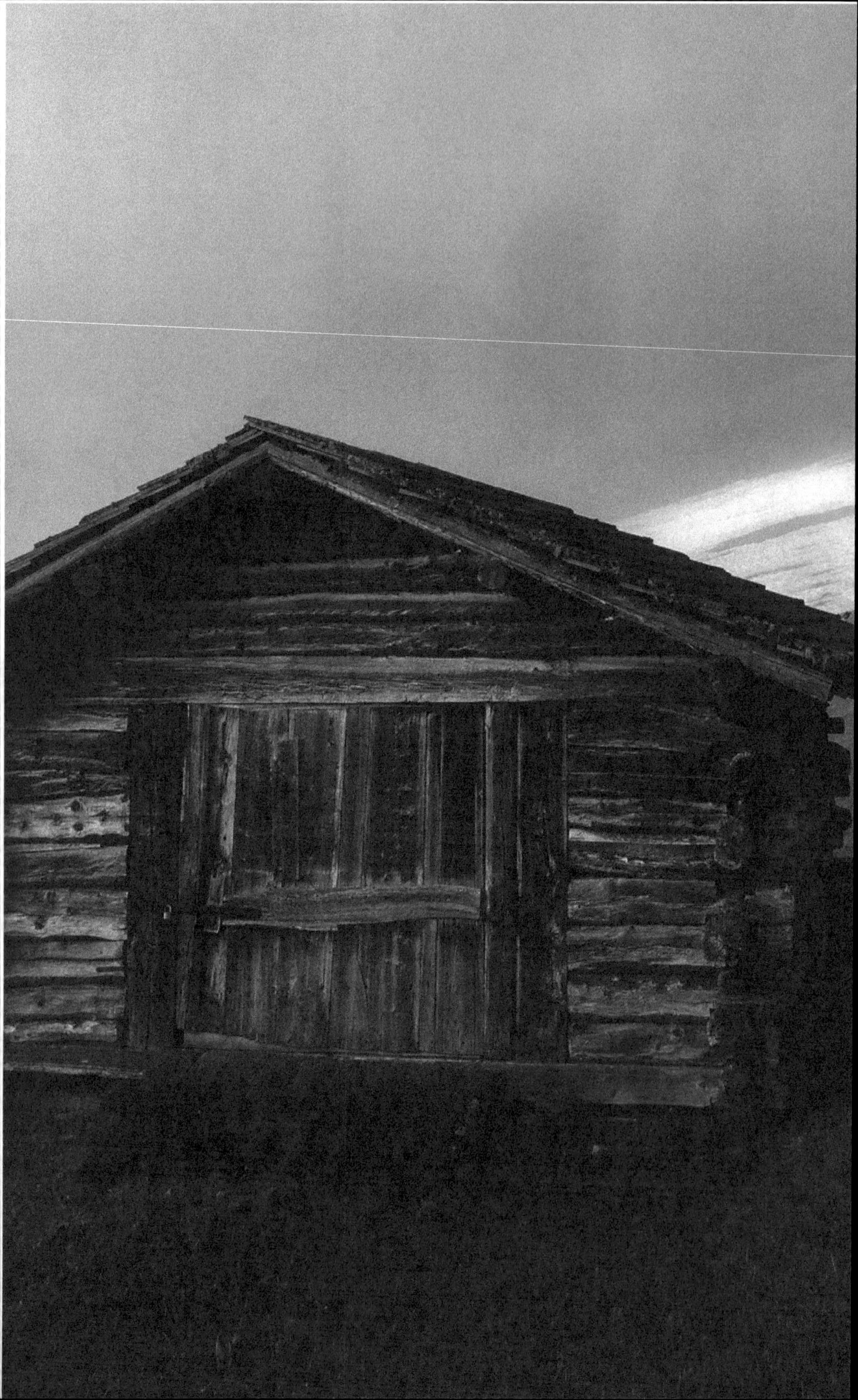

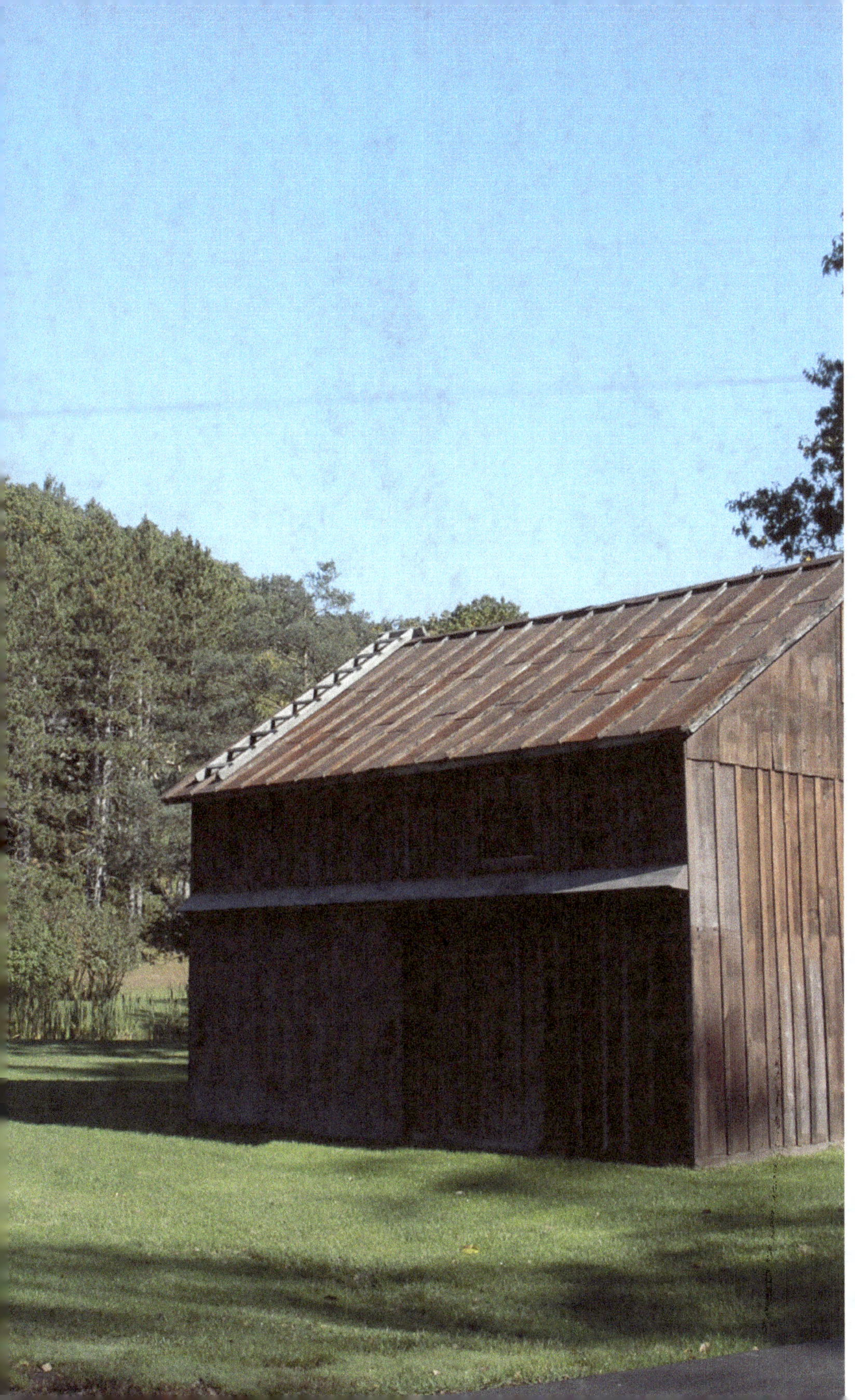

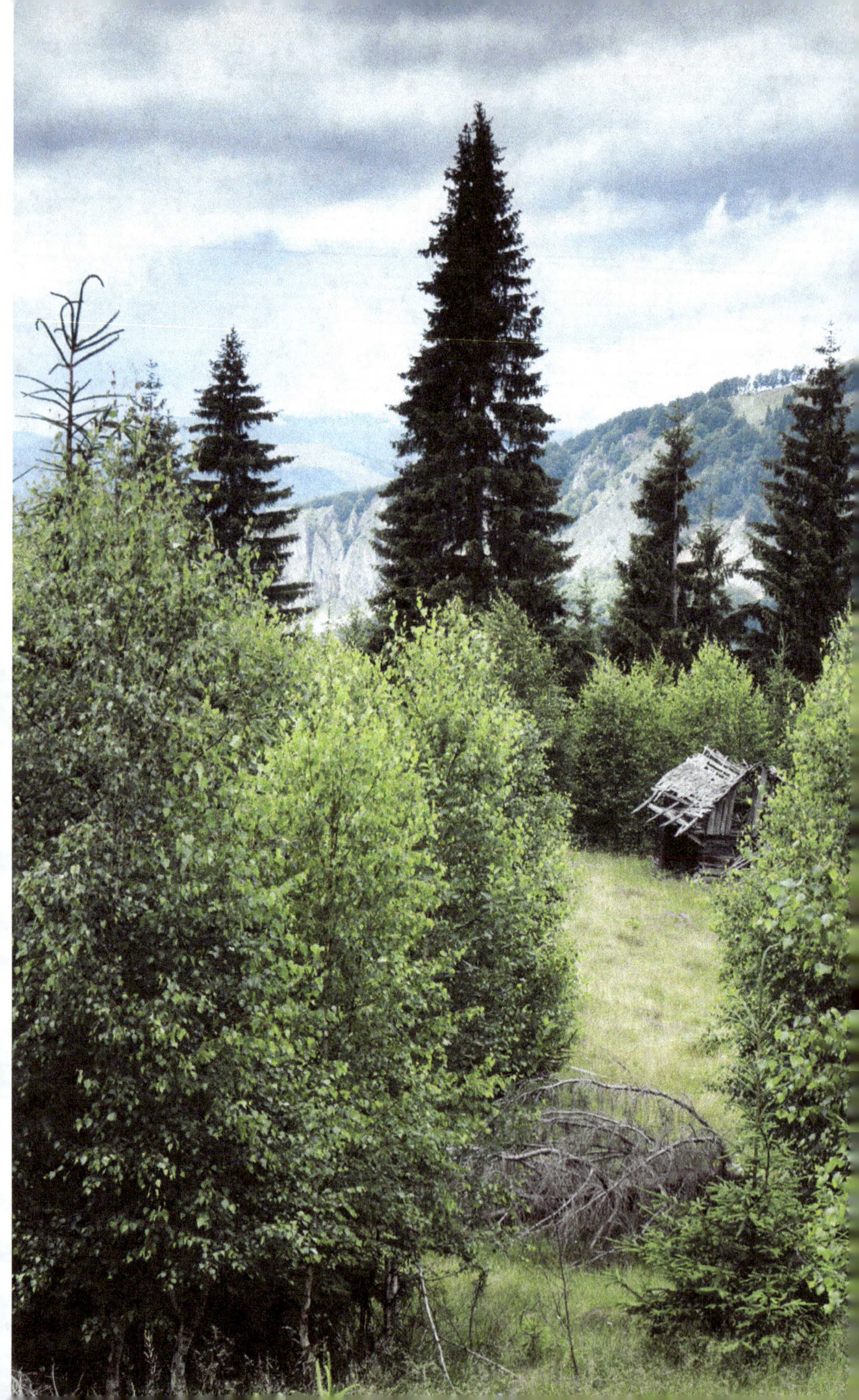

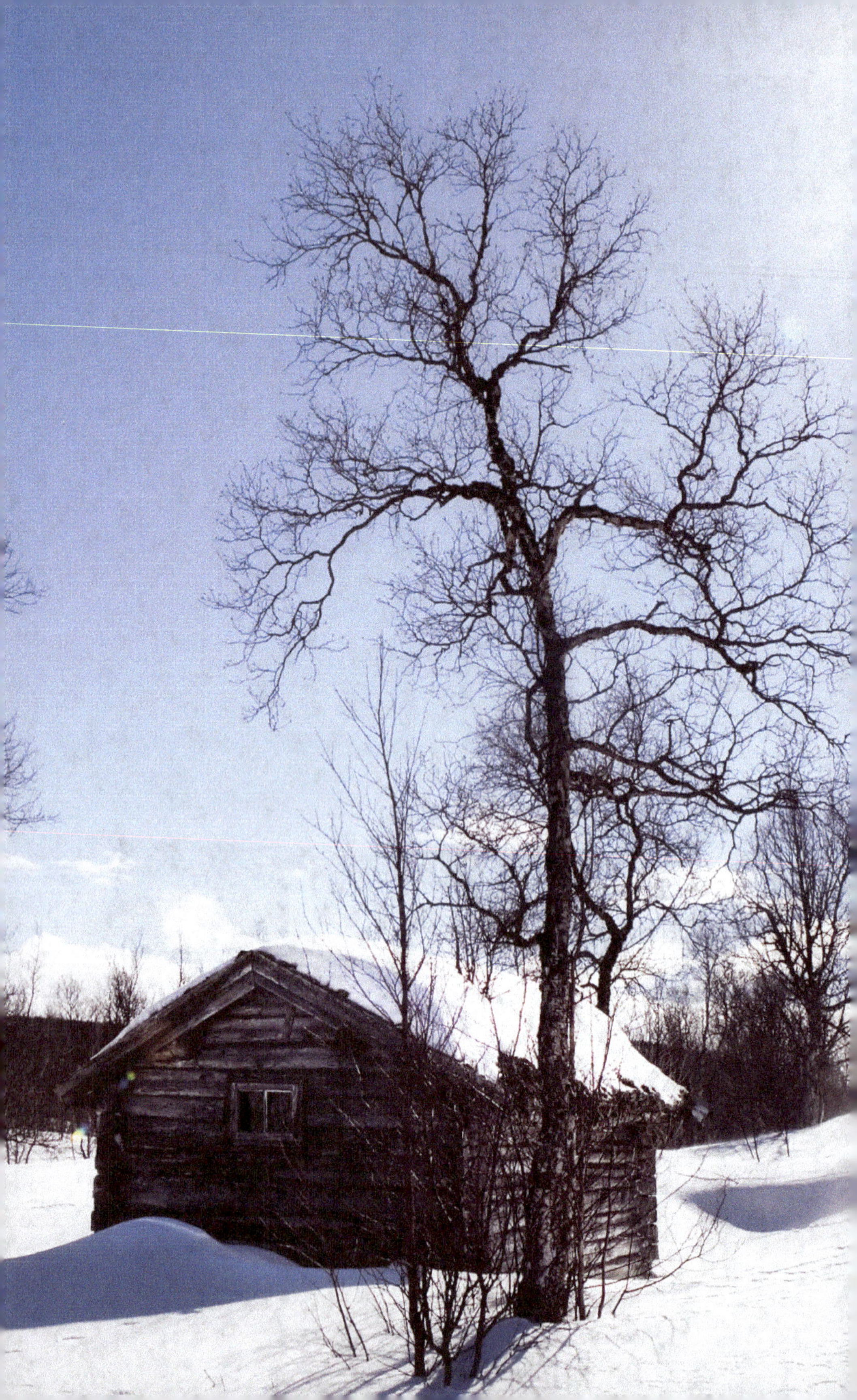

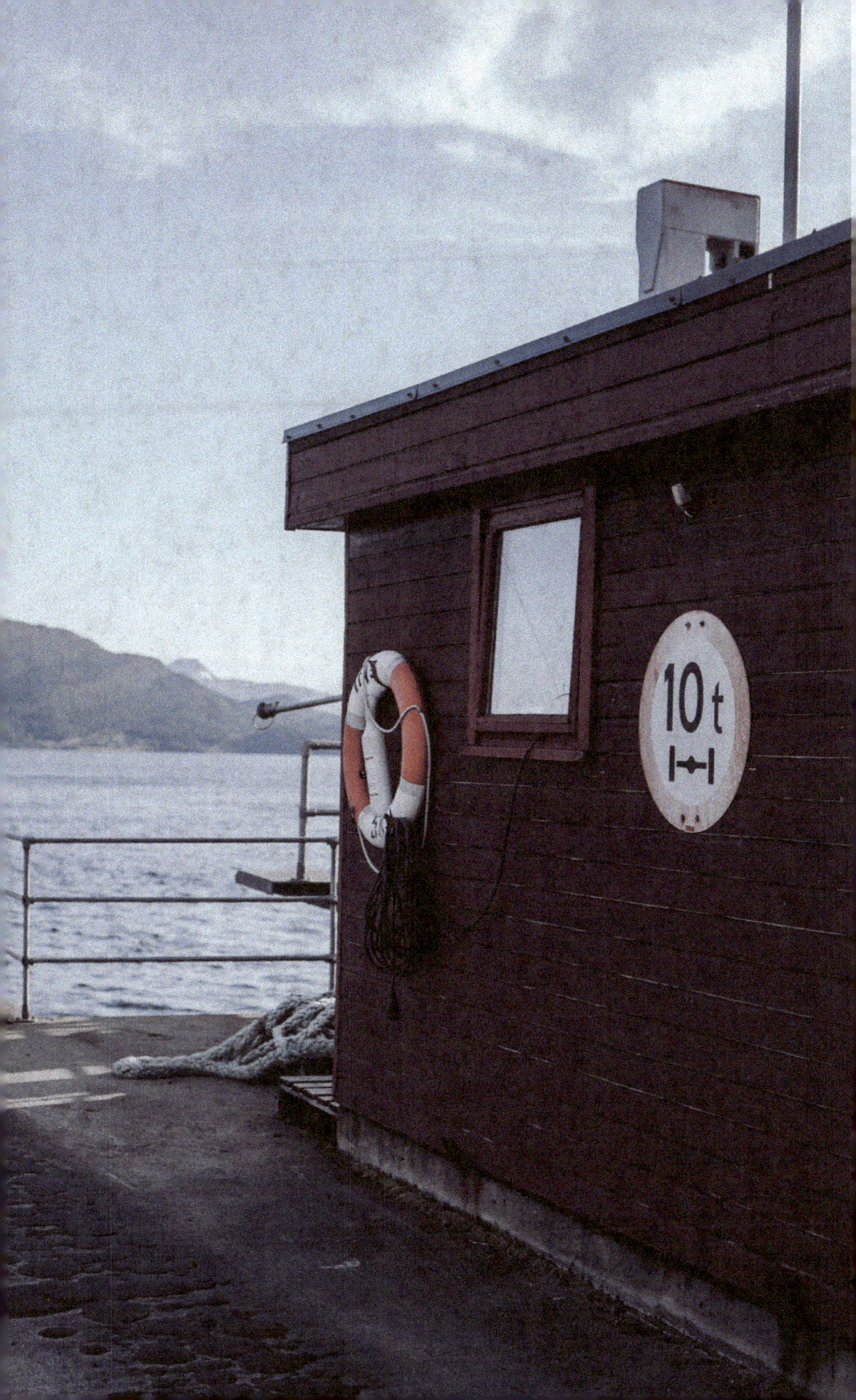

10 t

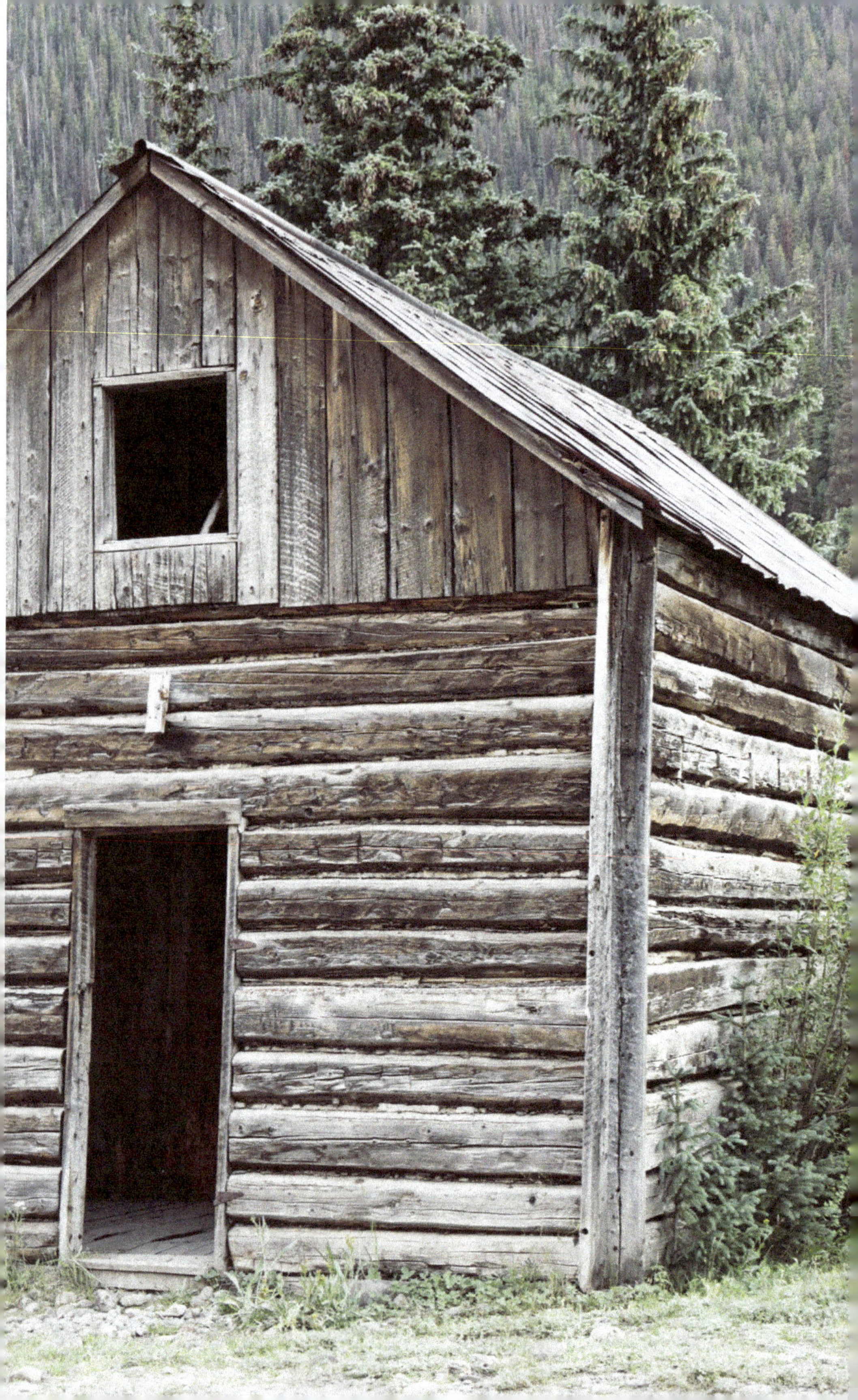

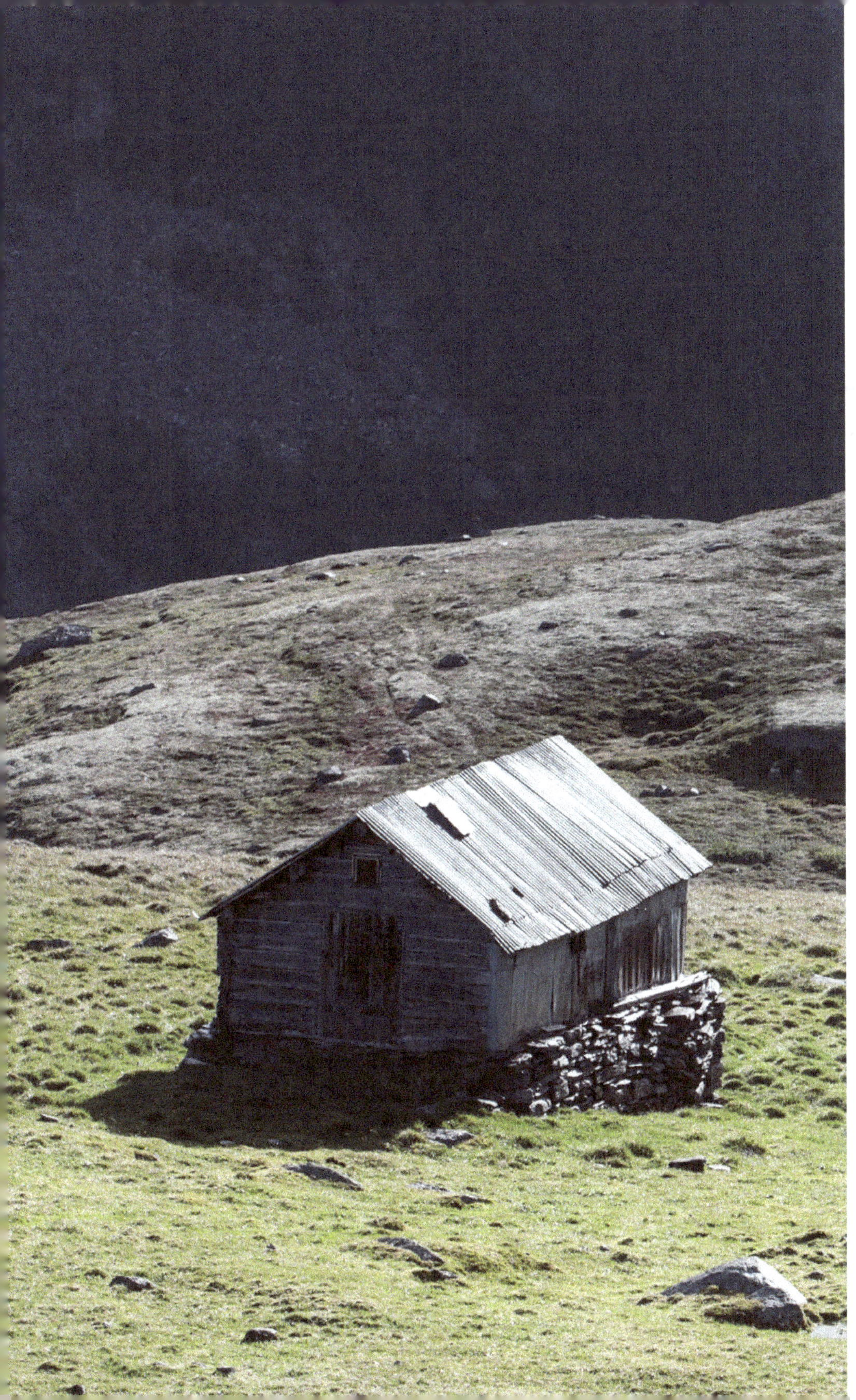

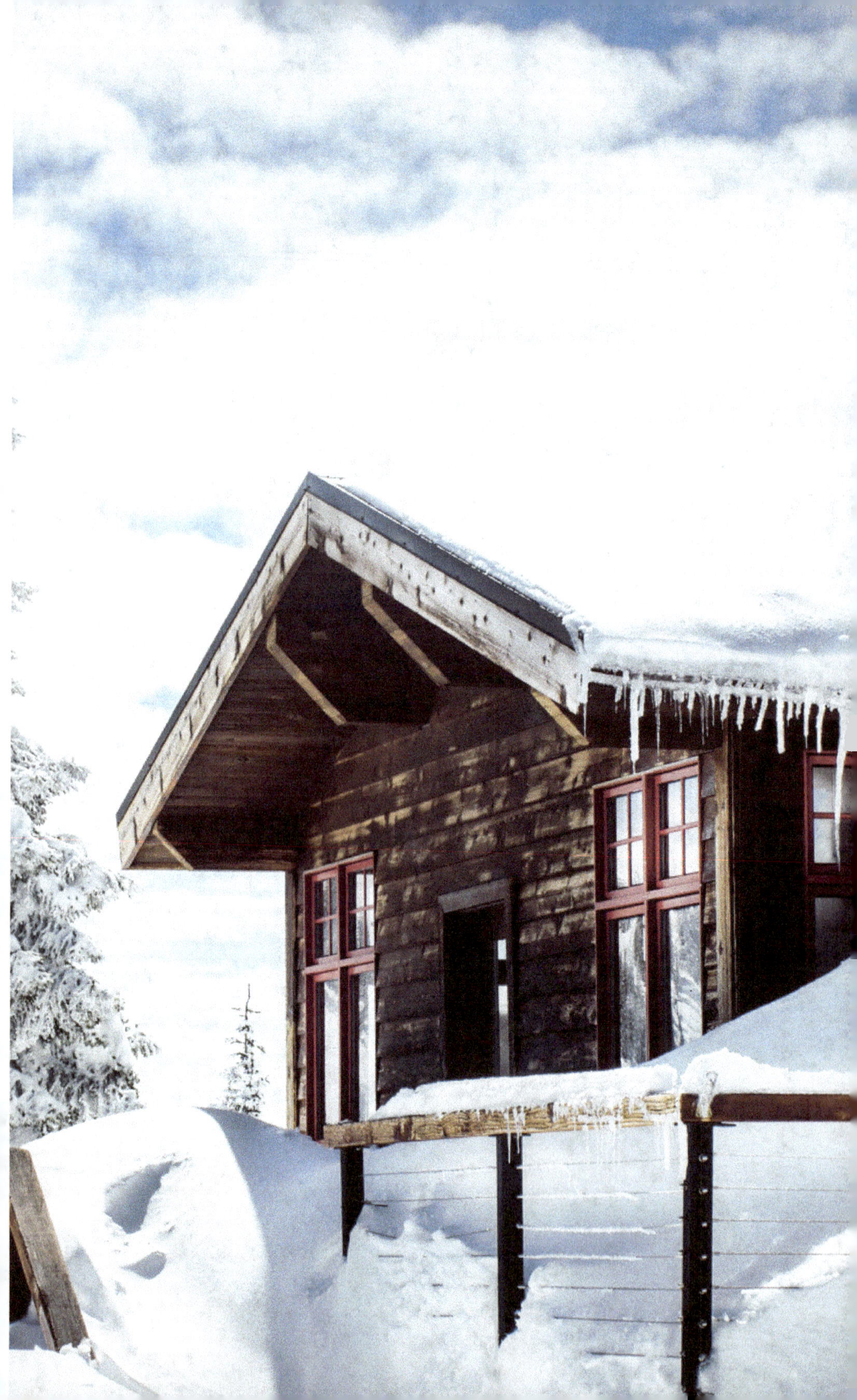

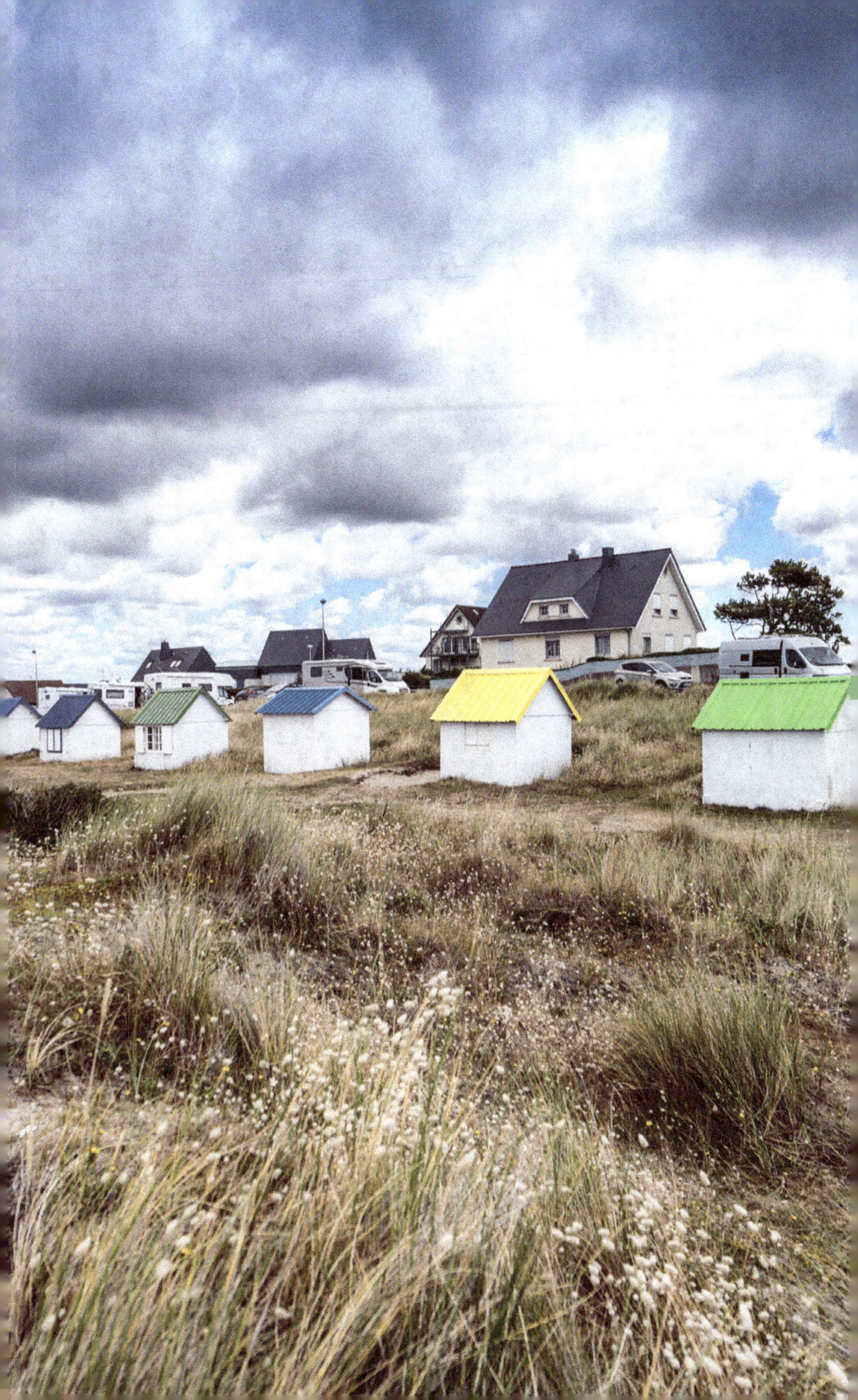

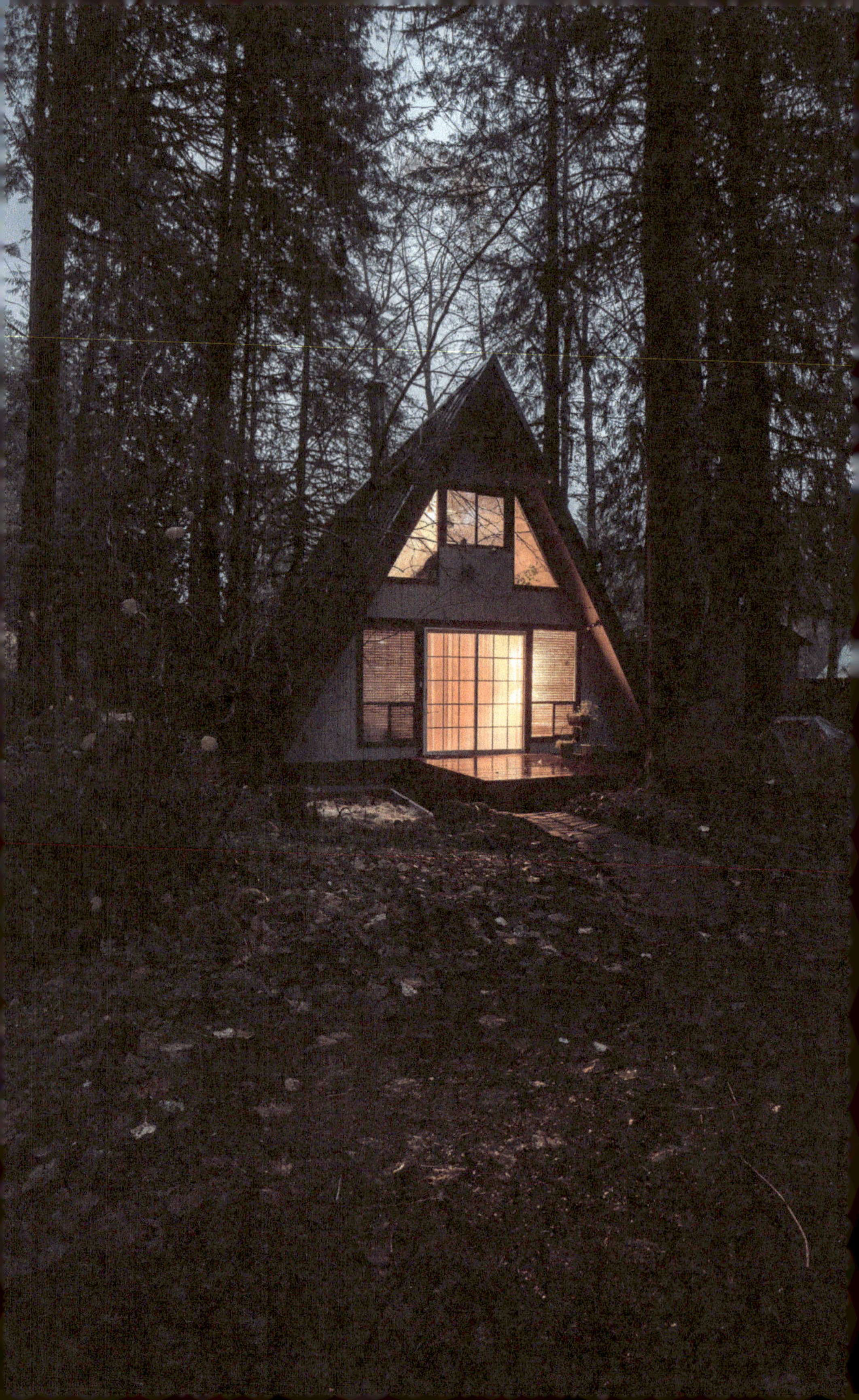

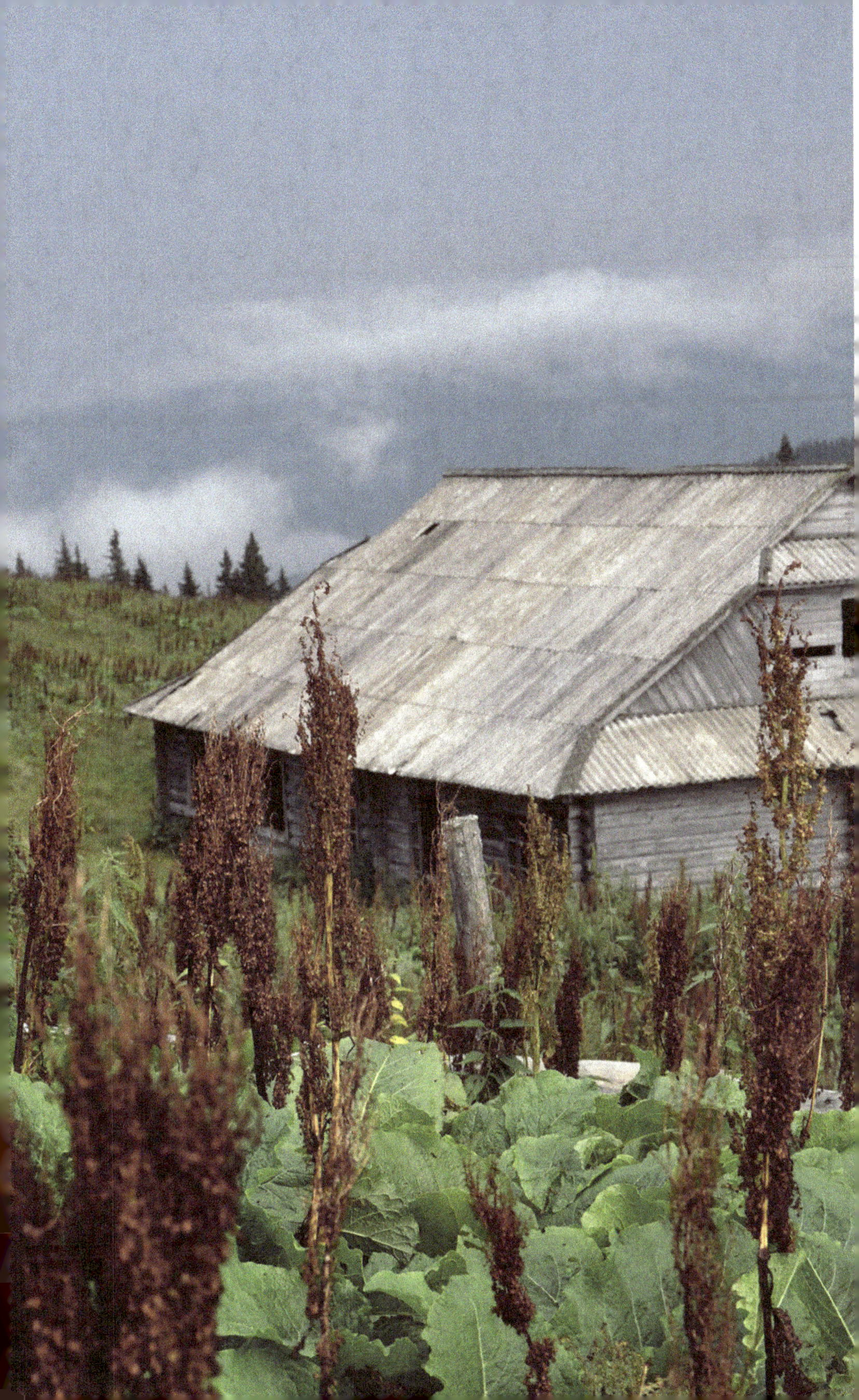

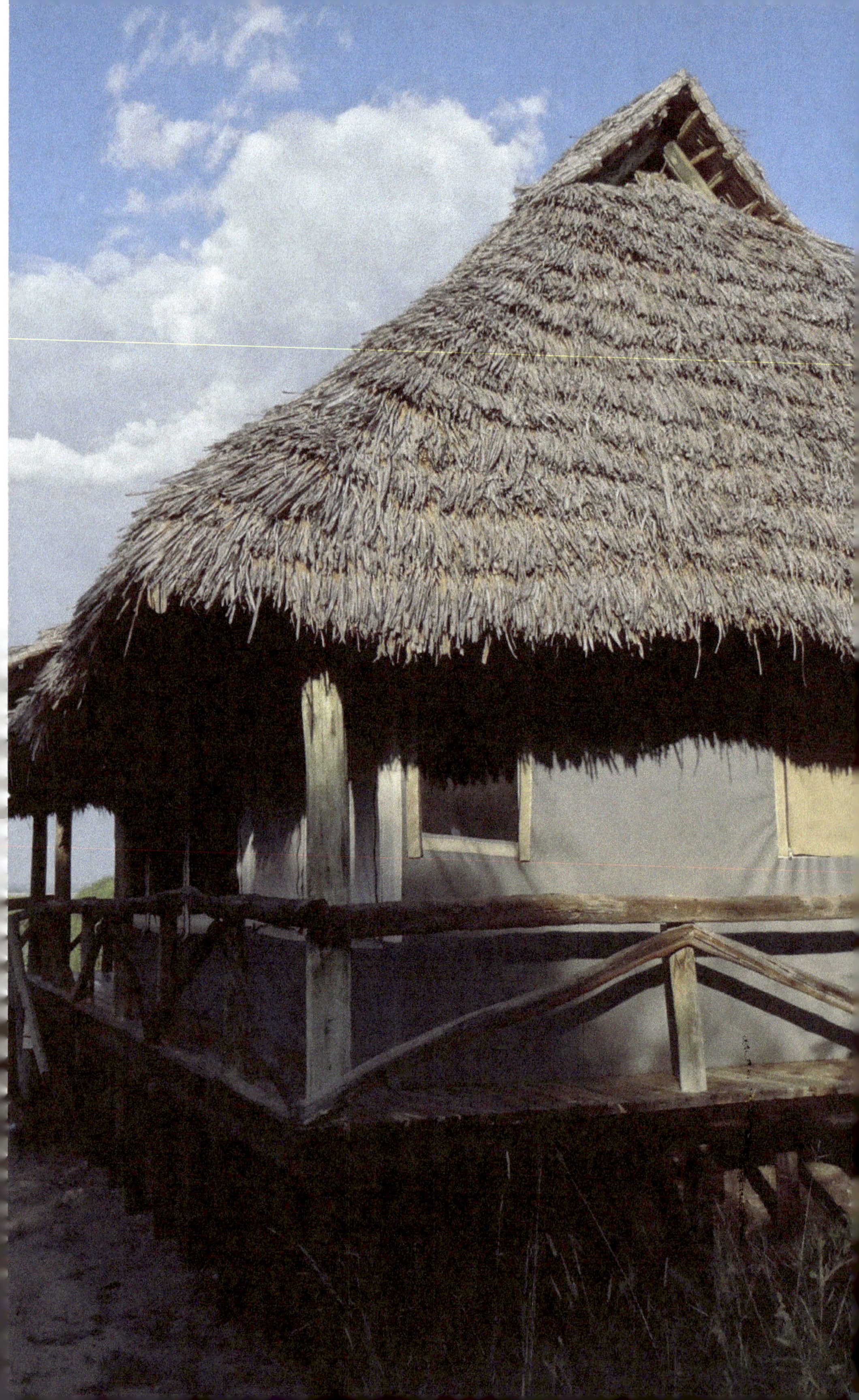

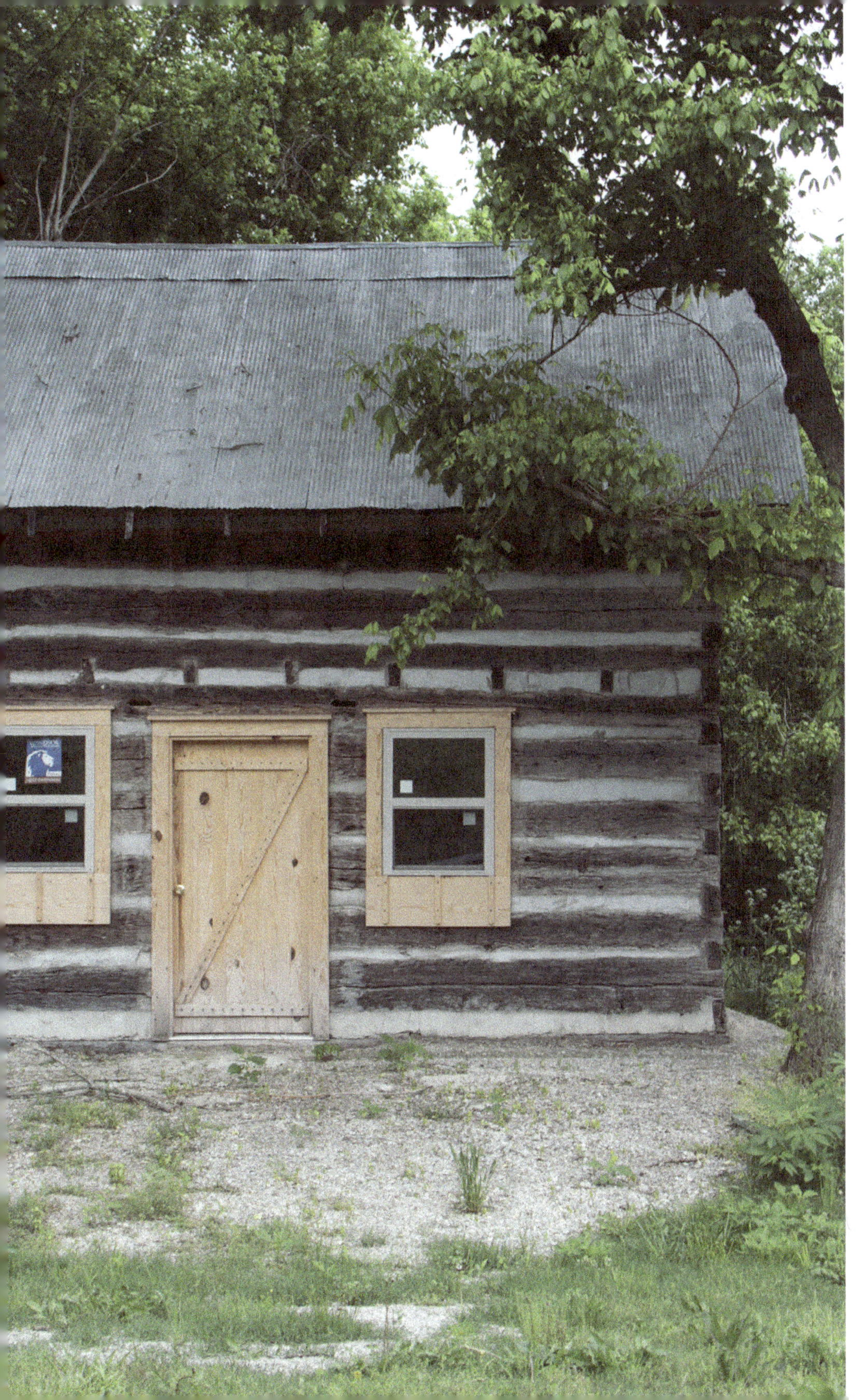

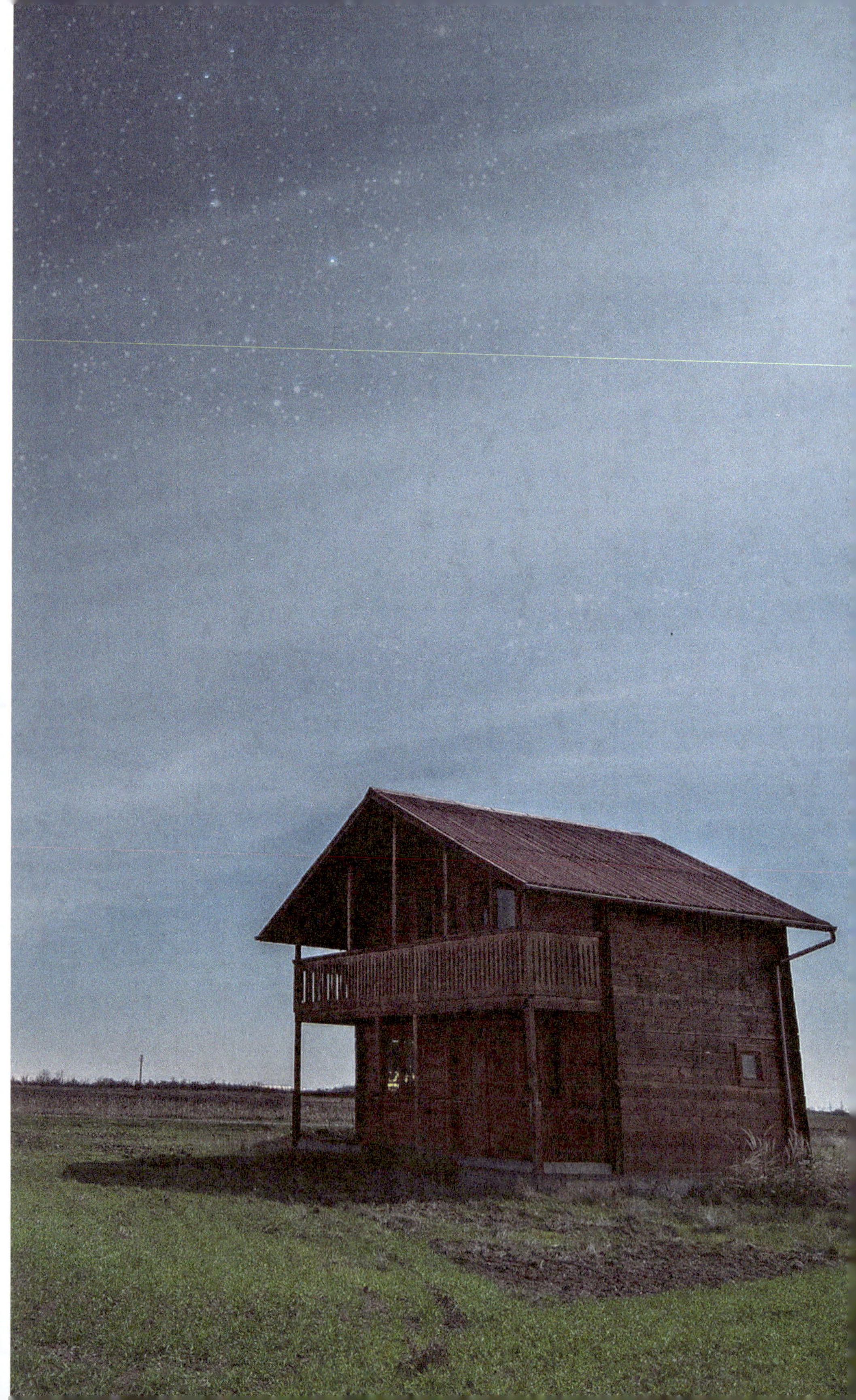

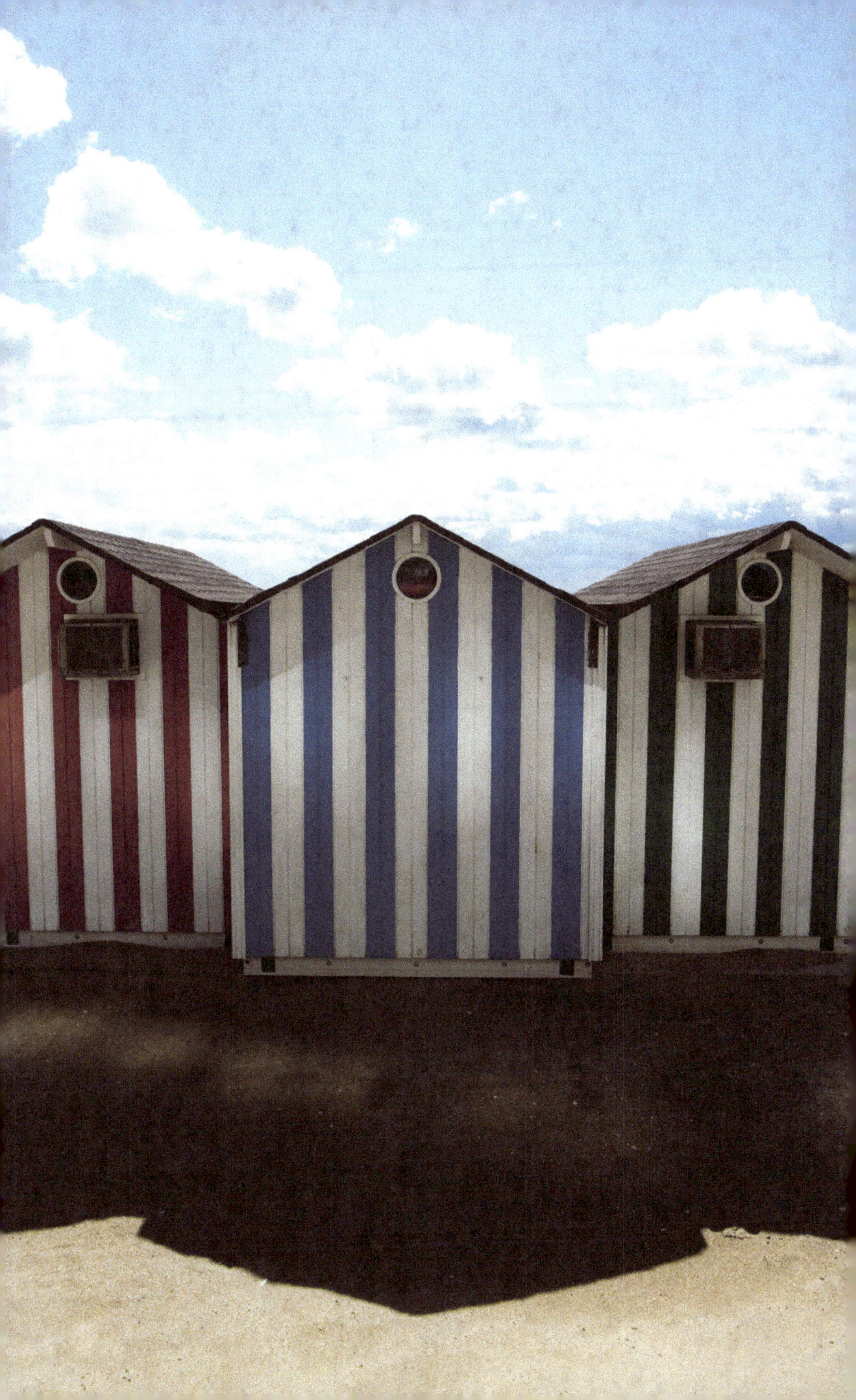

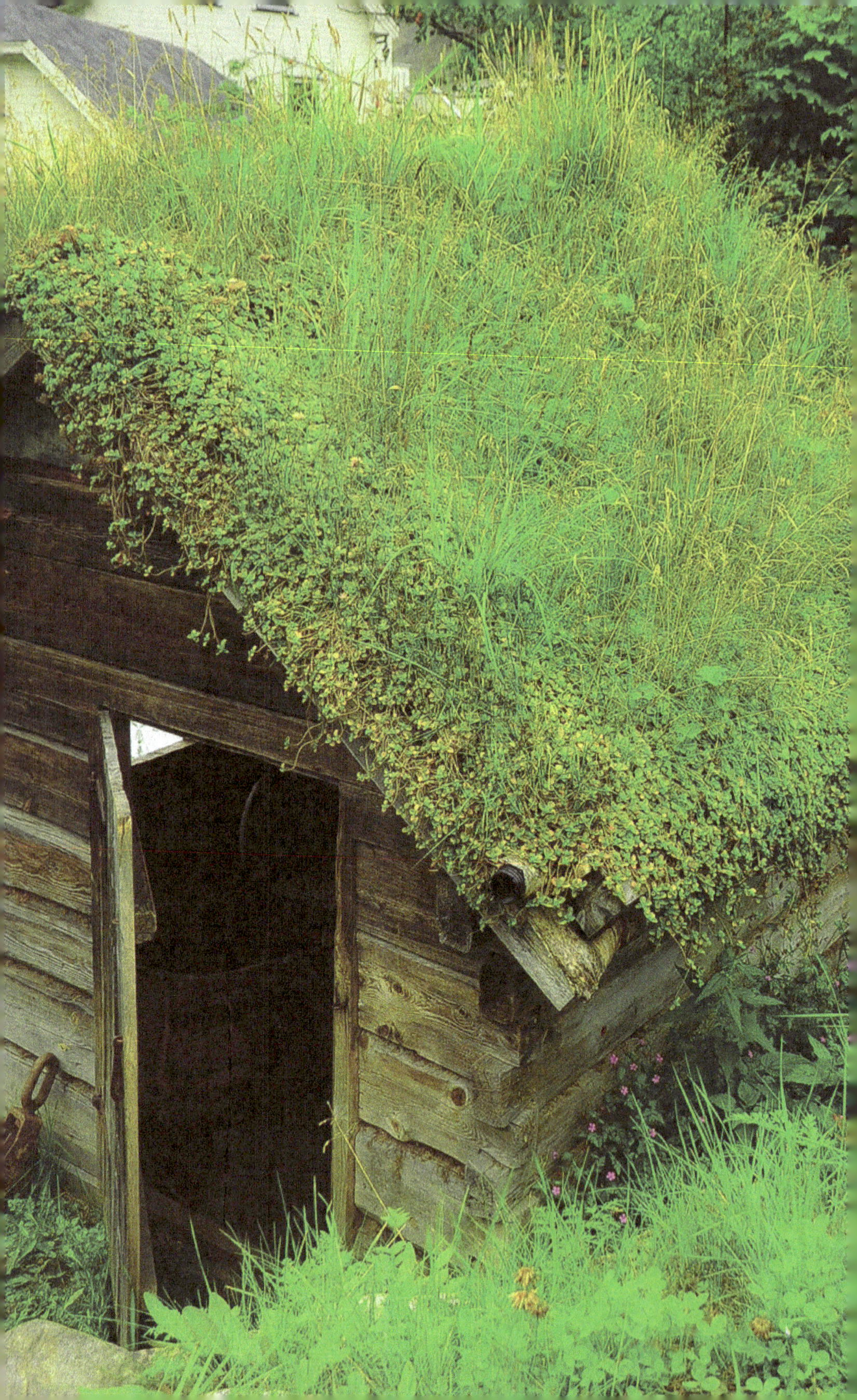

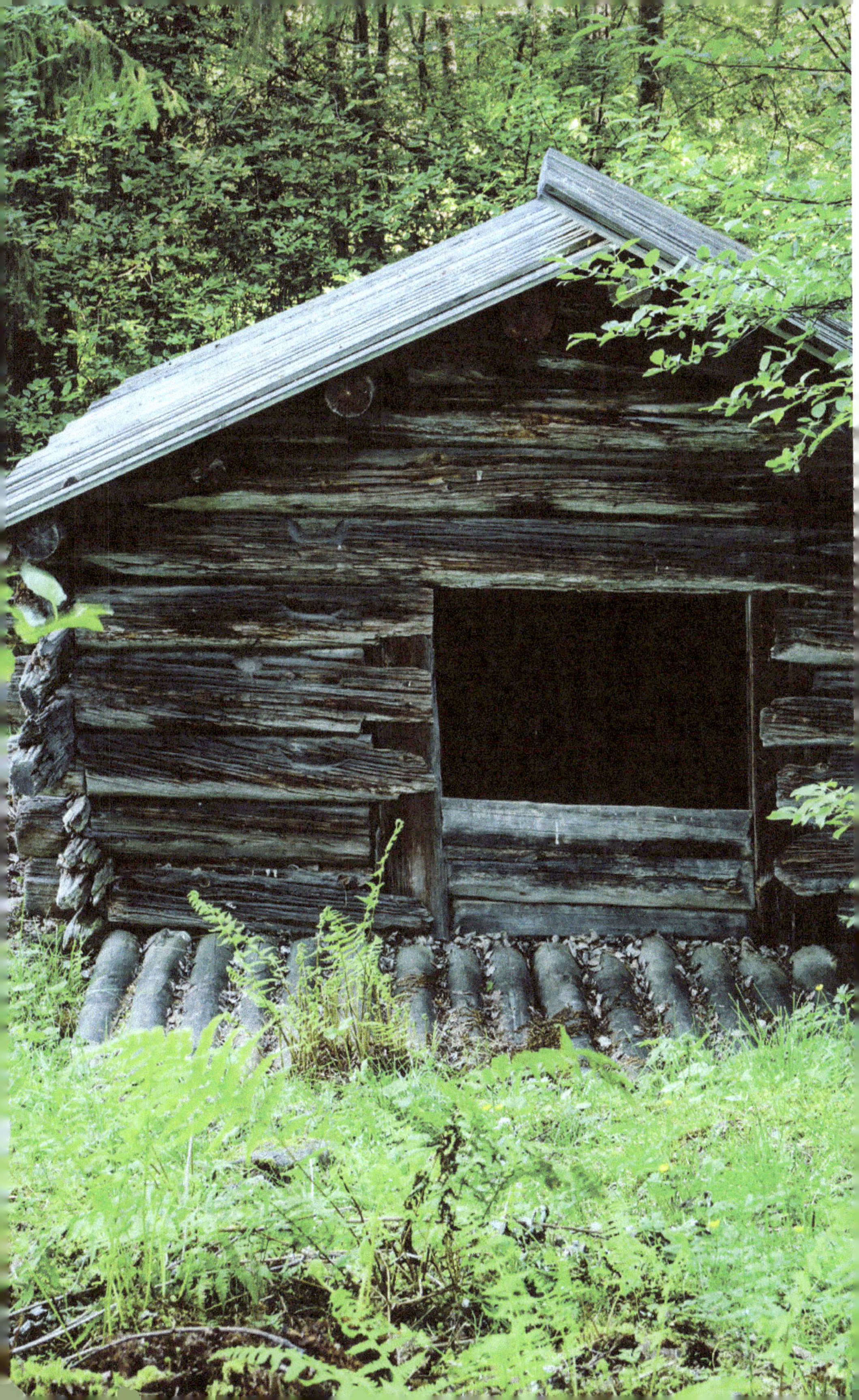

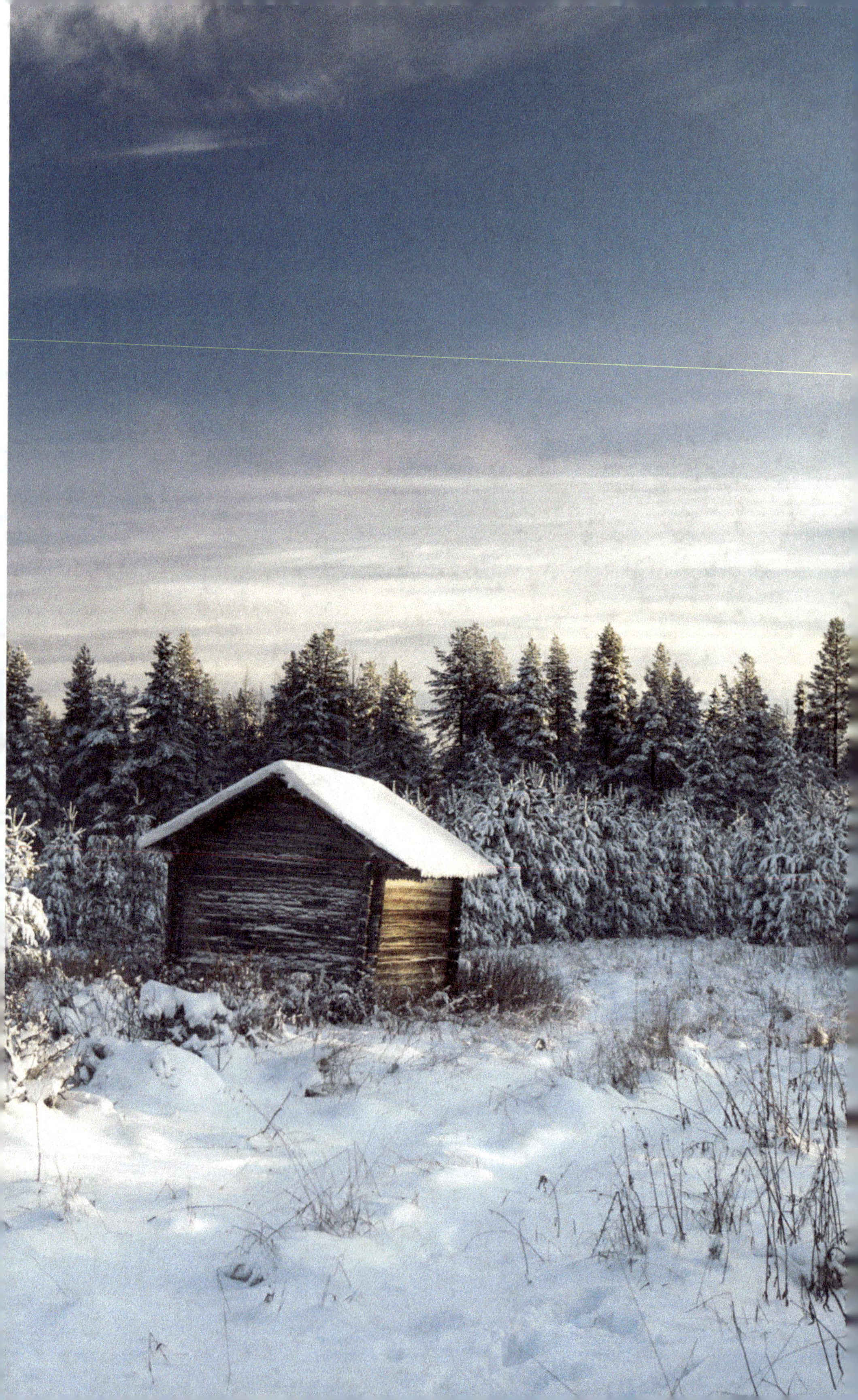

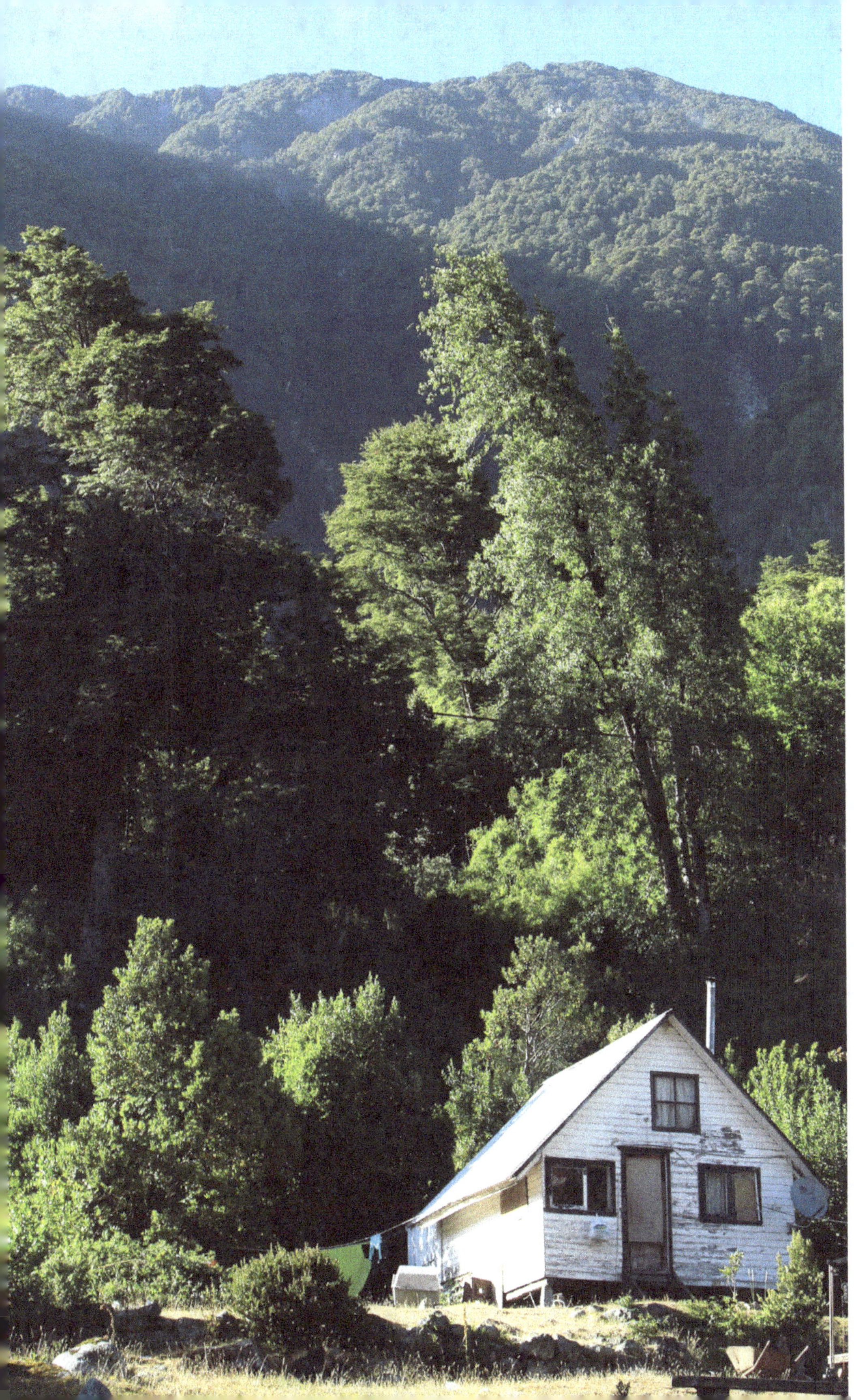

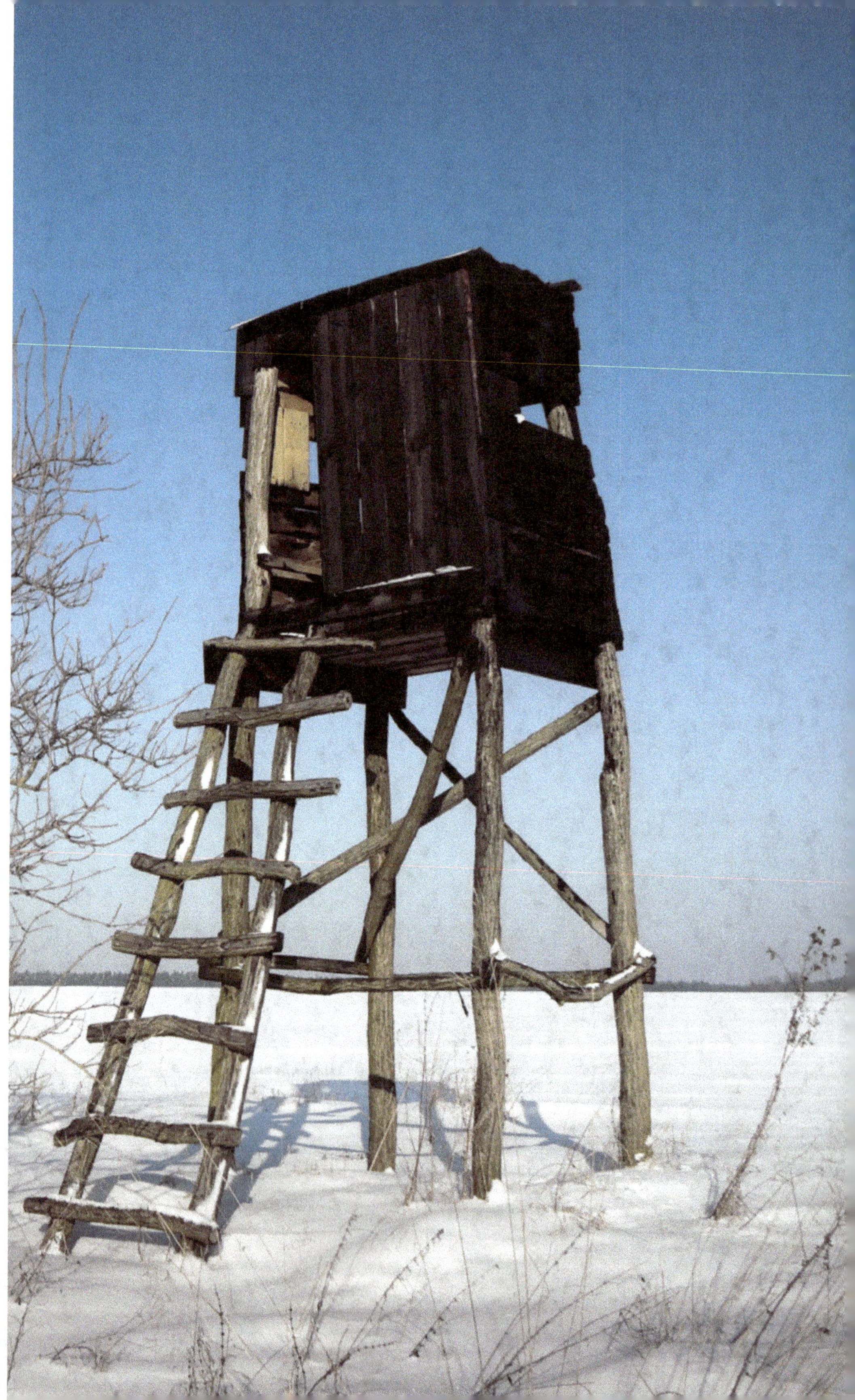

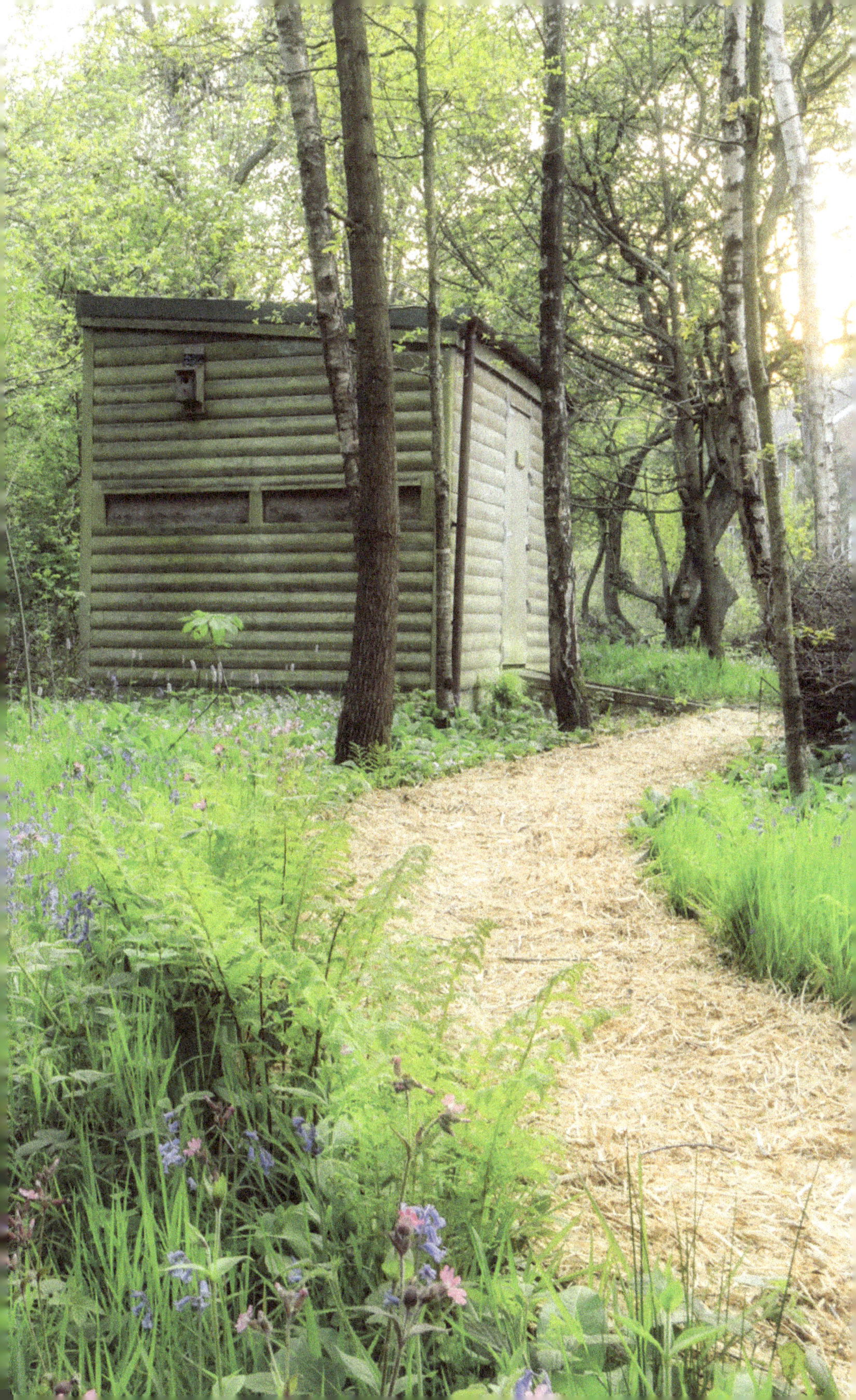

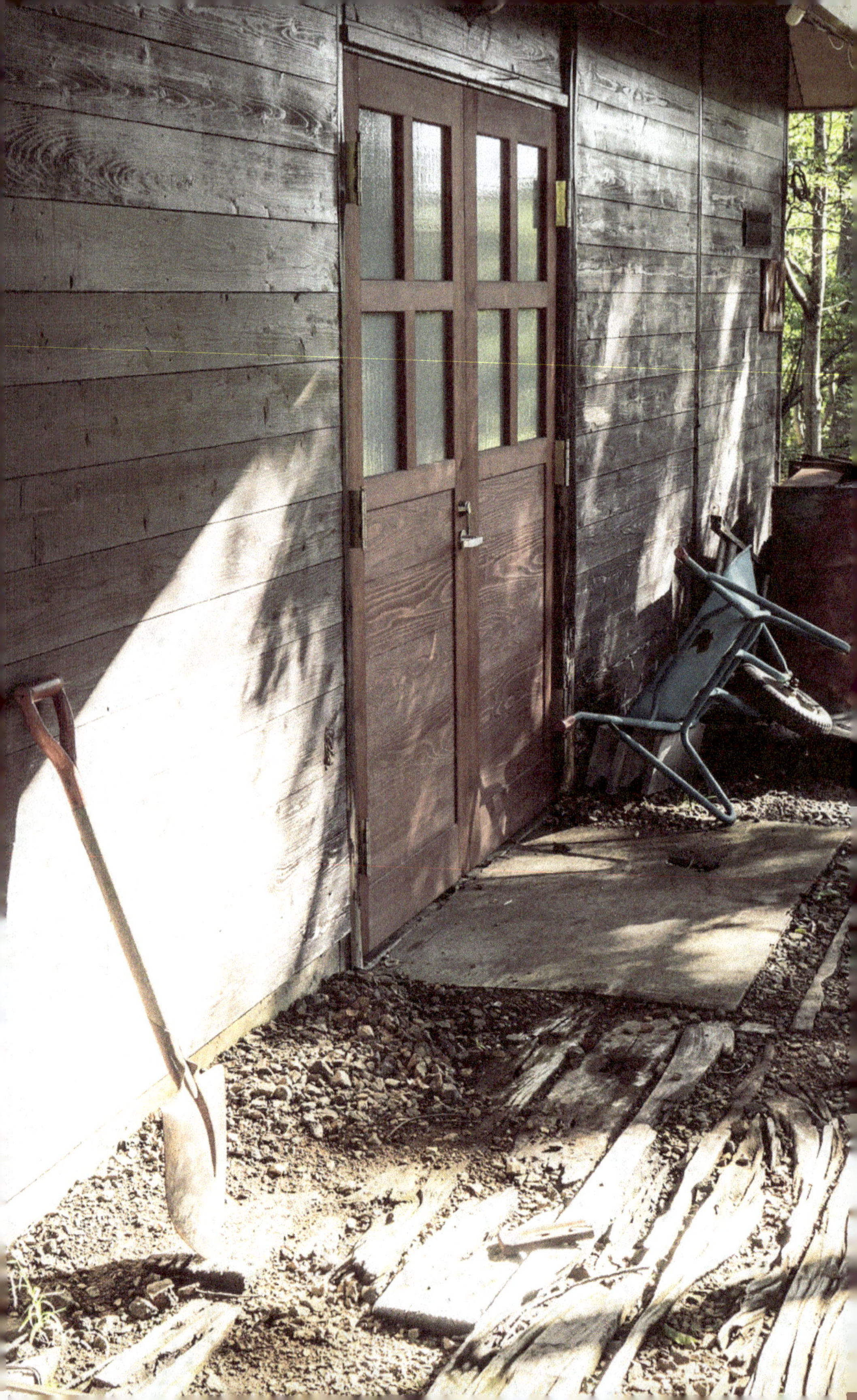

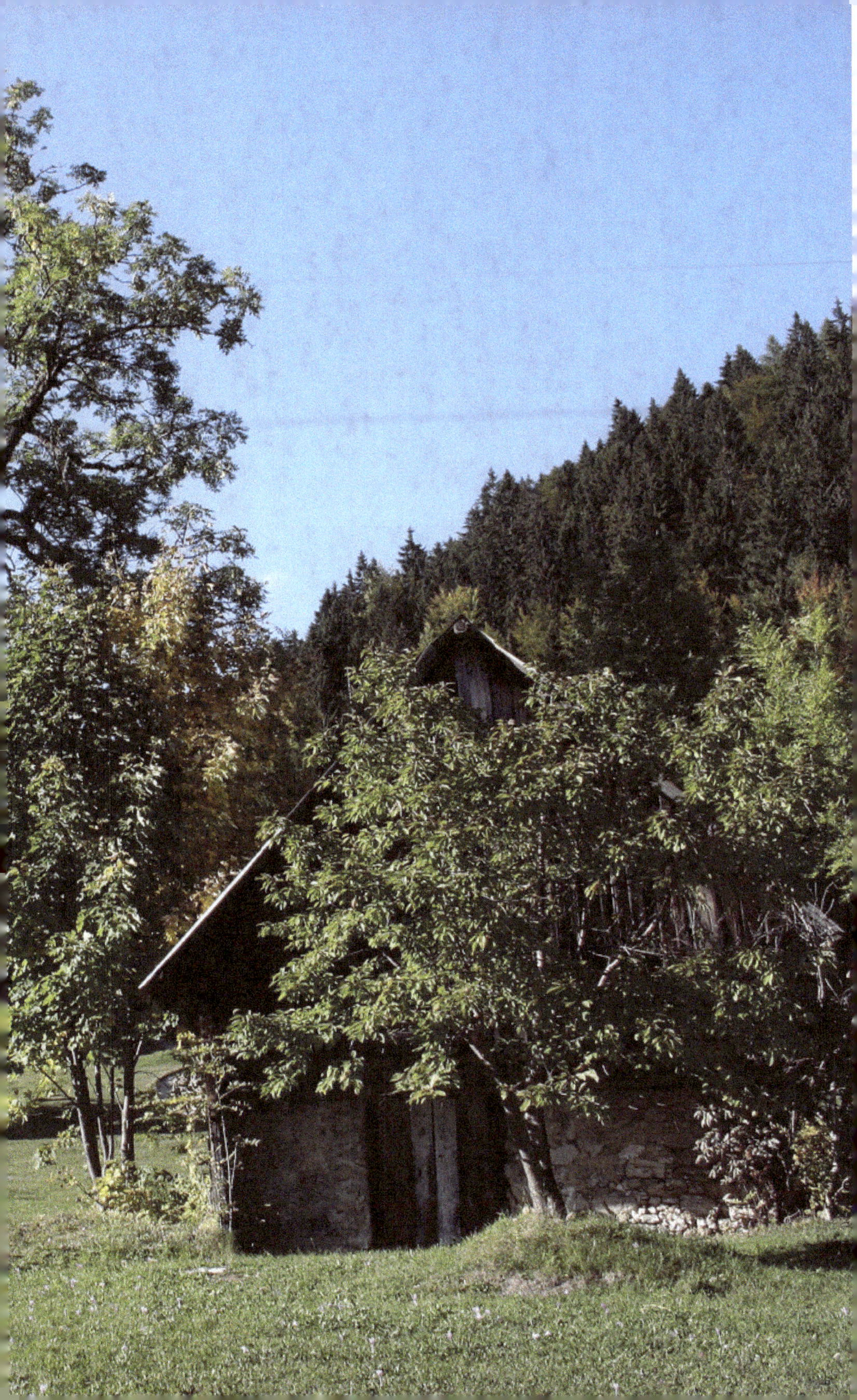

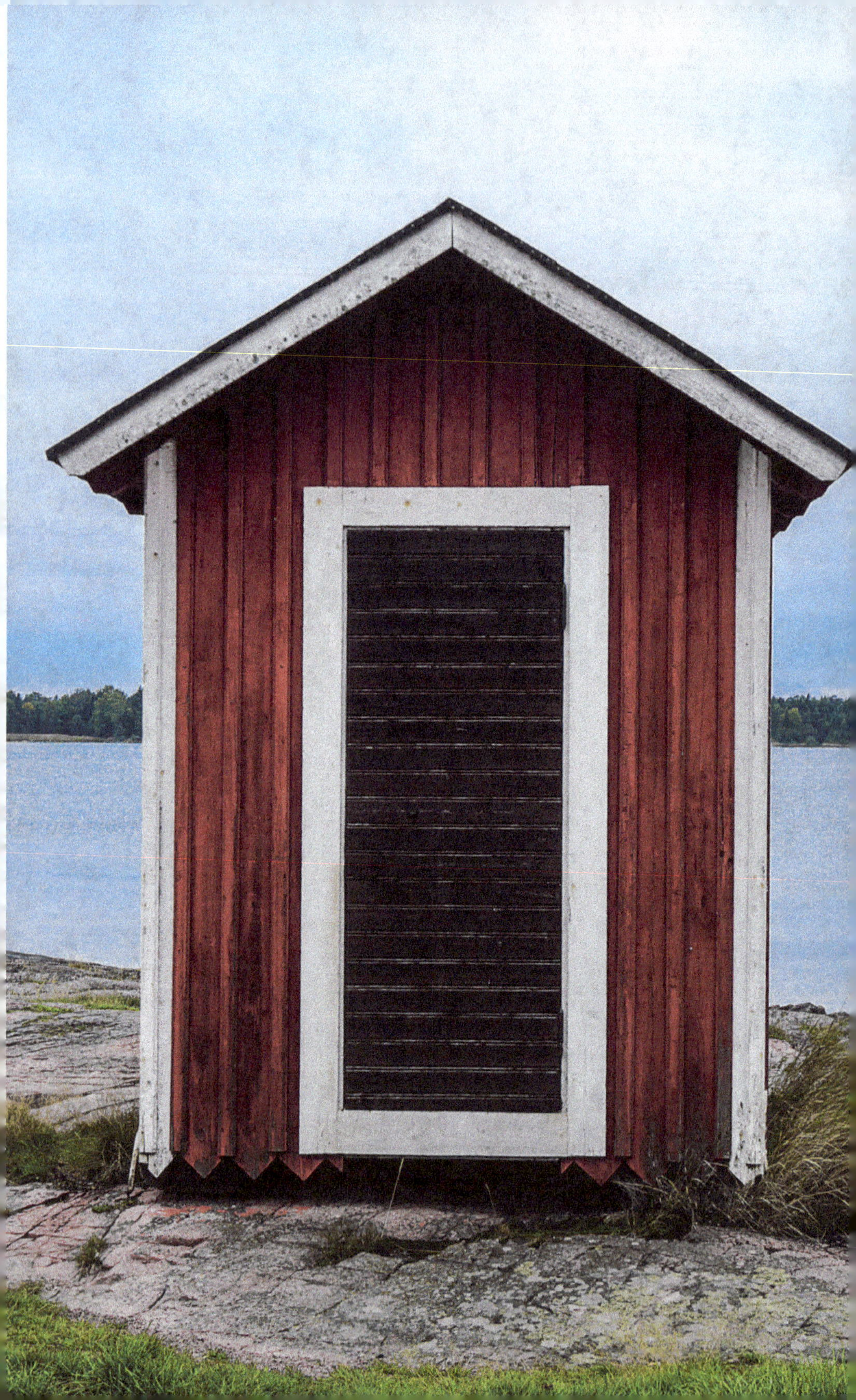

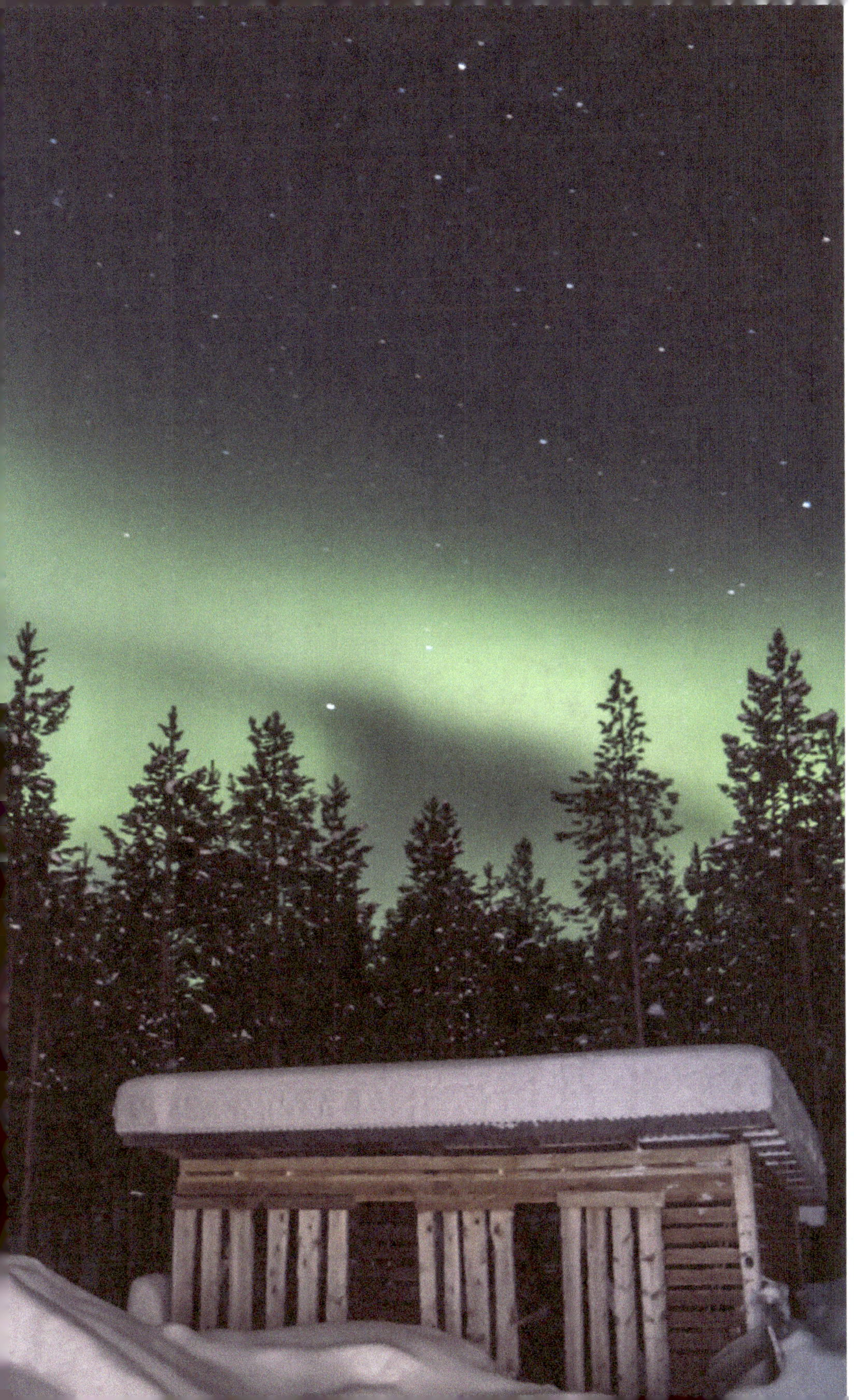

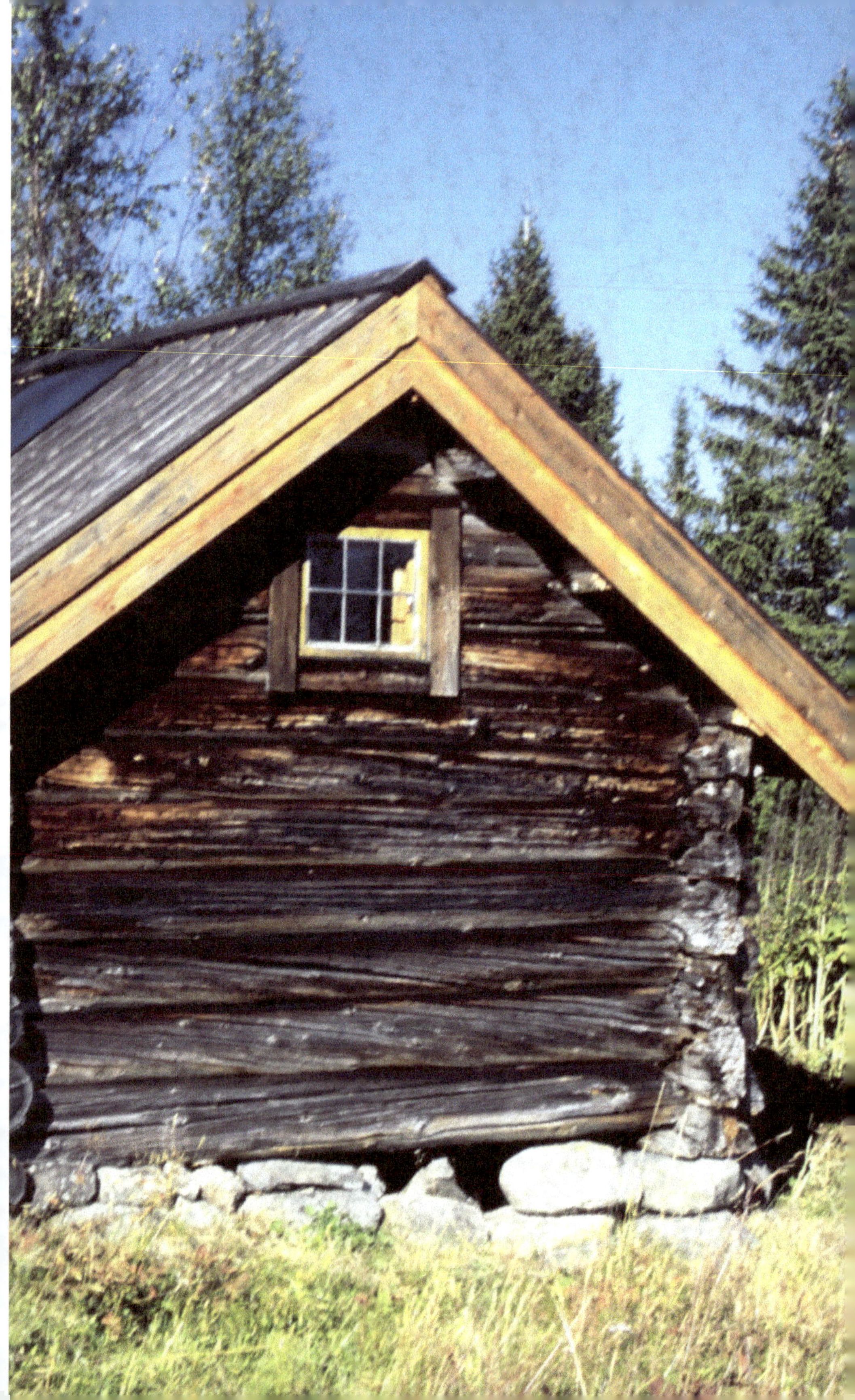

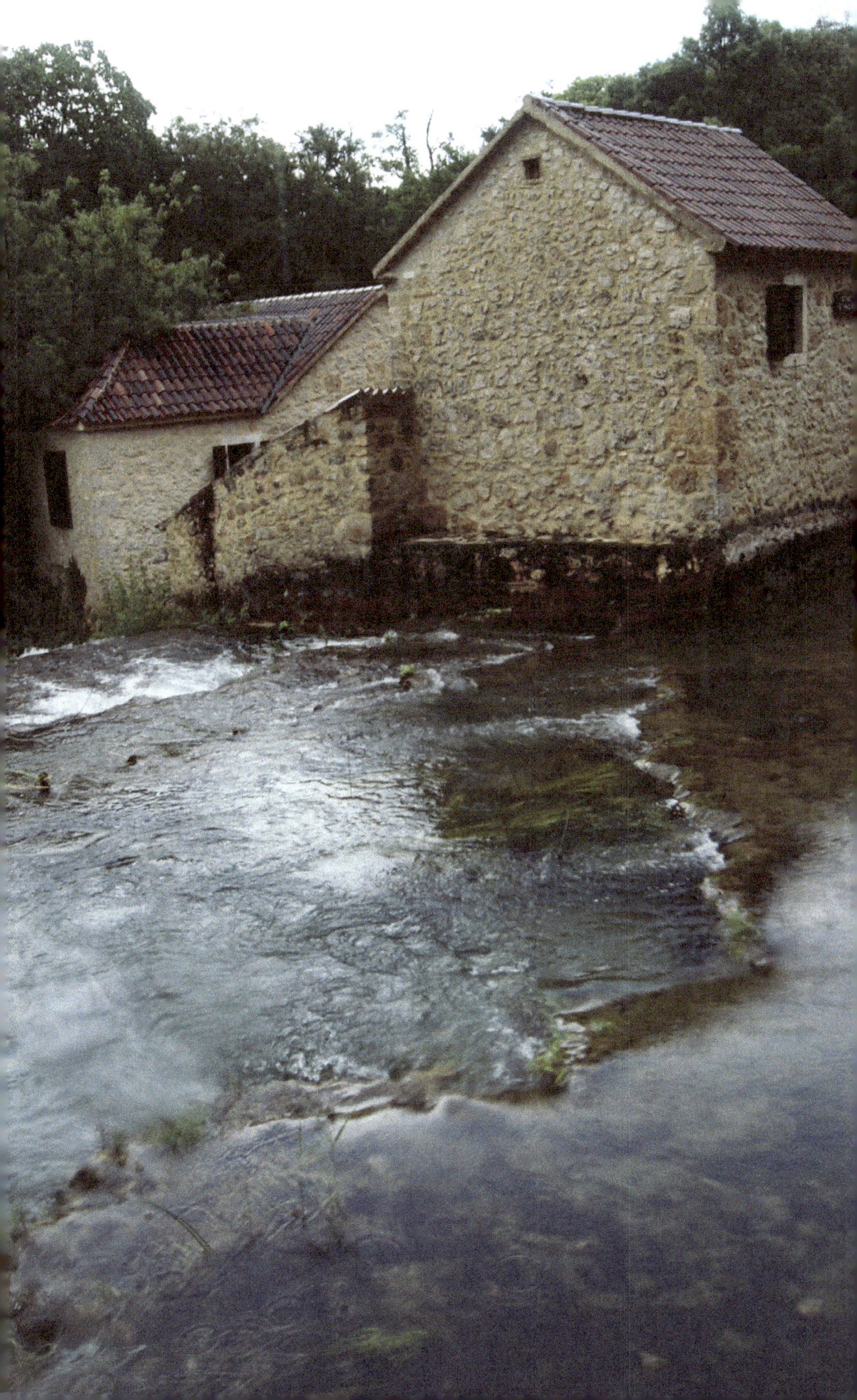

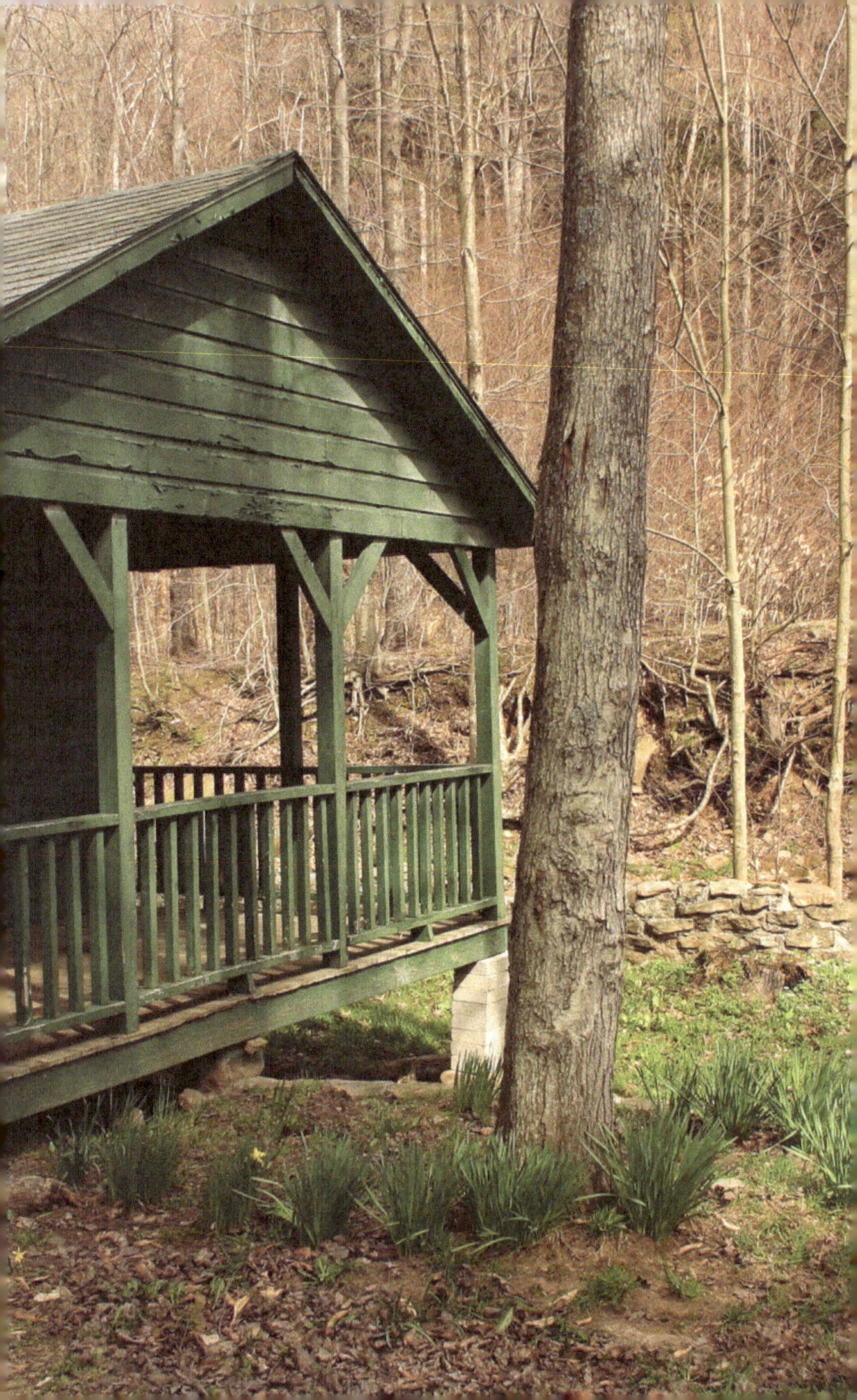

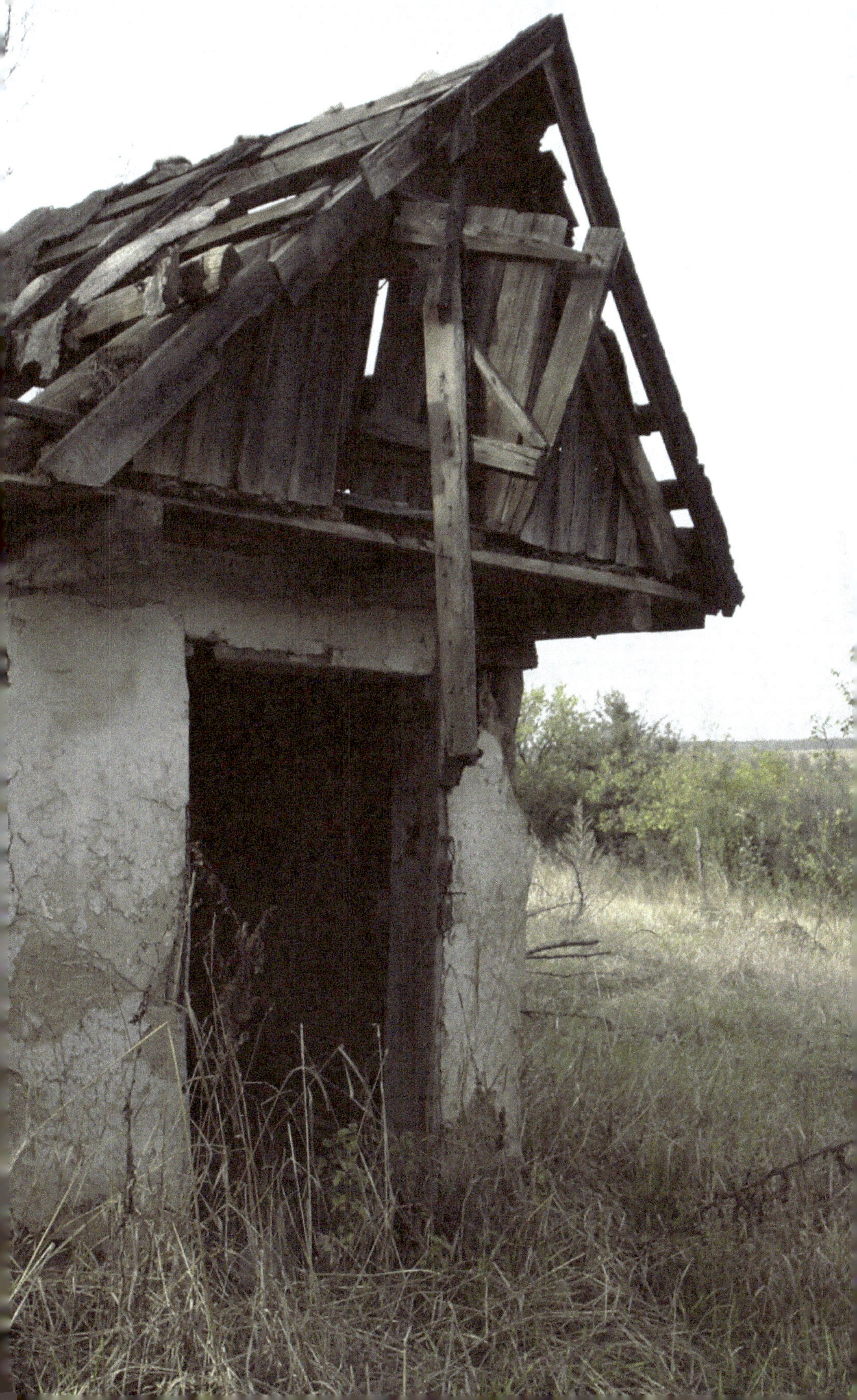

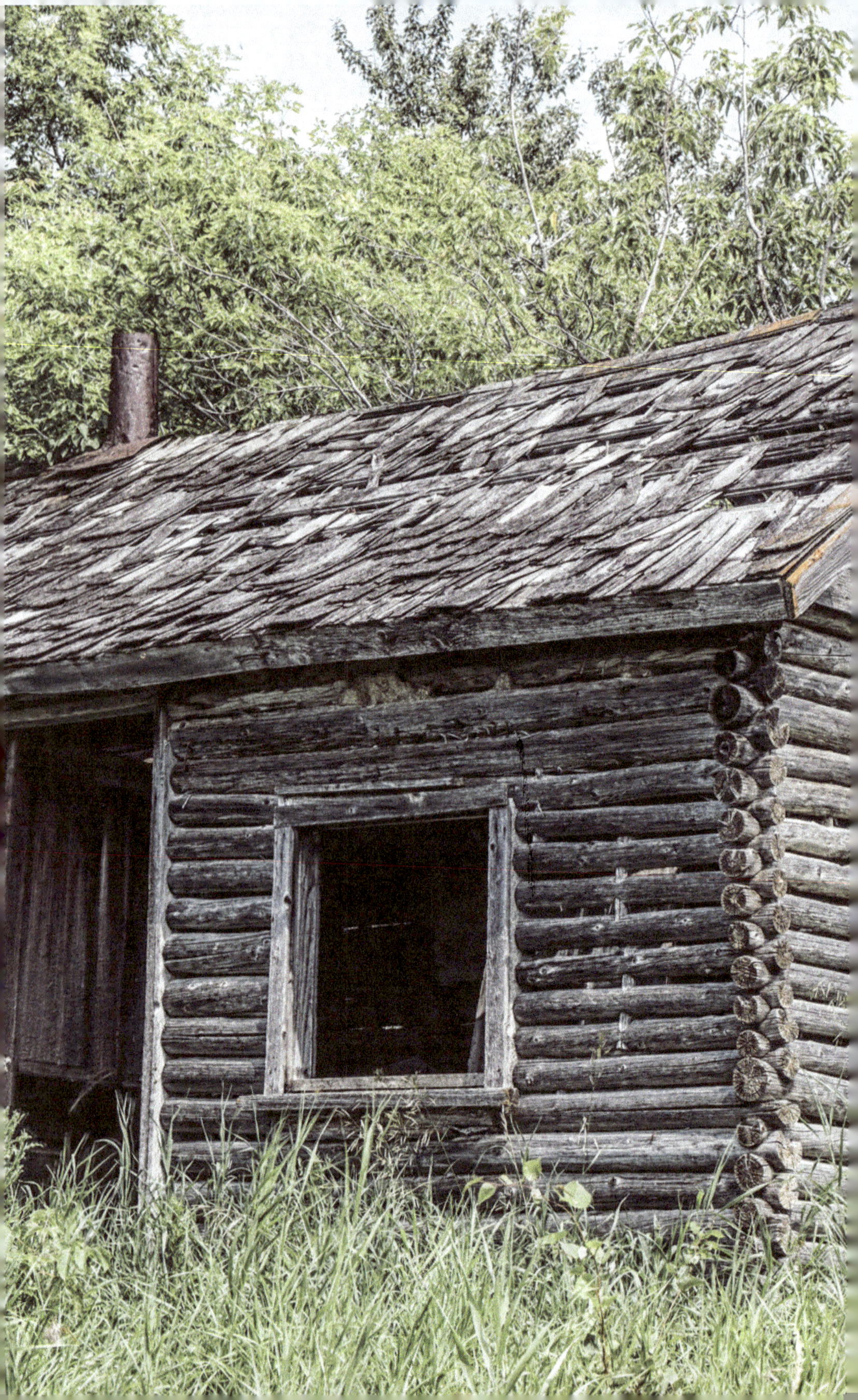

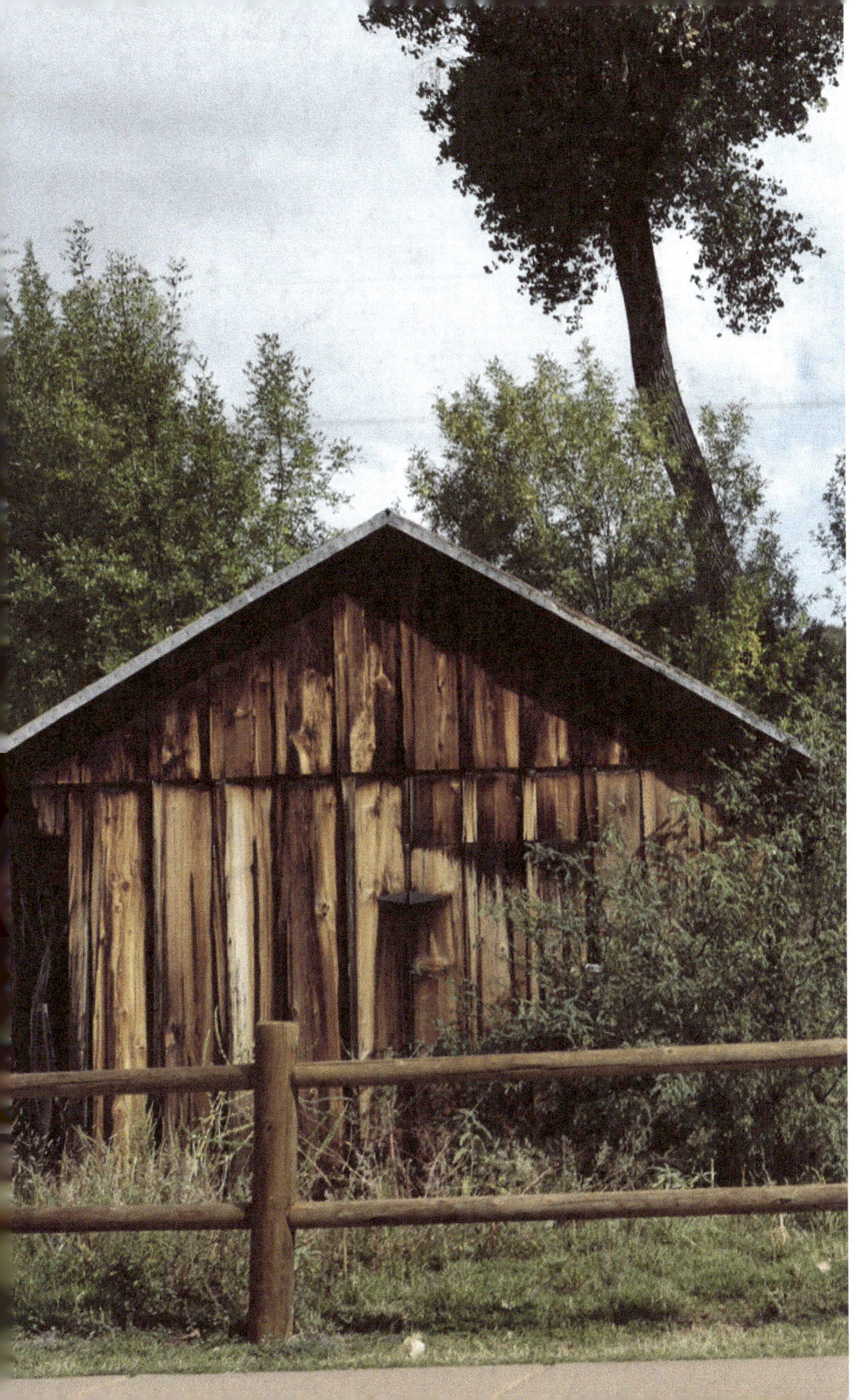

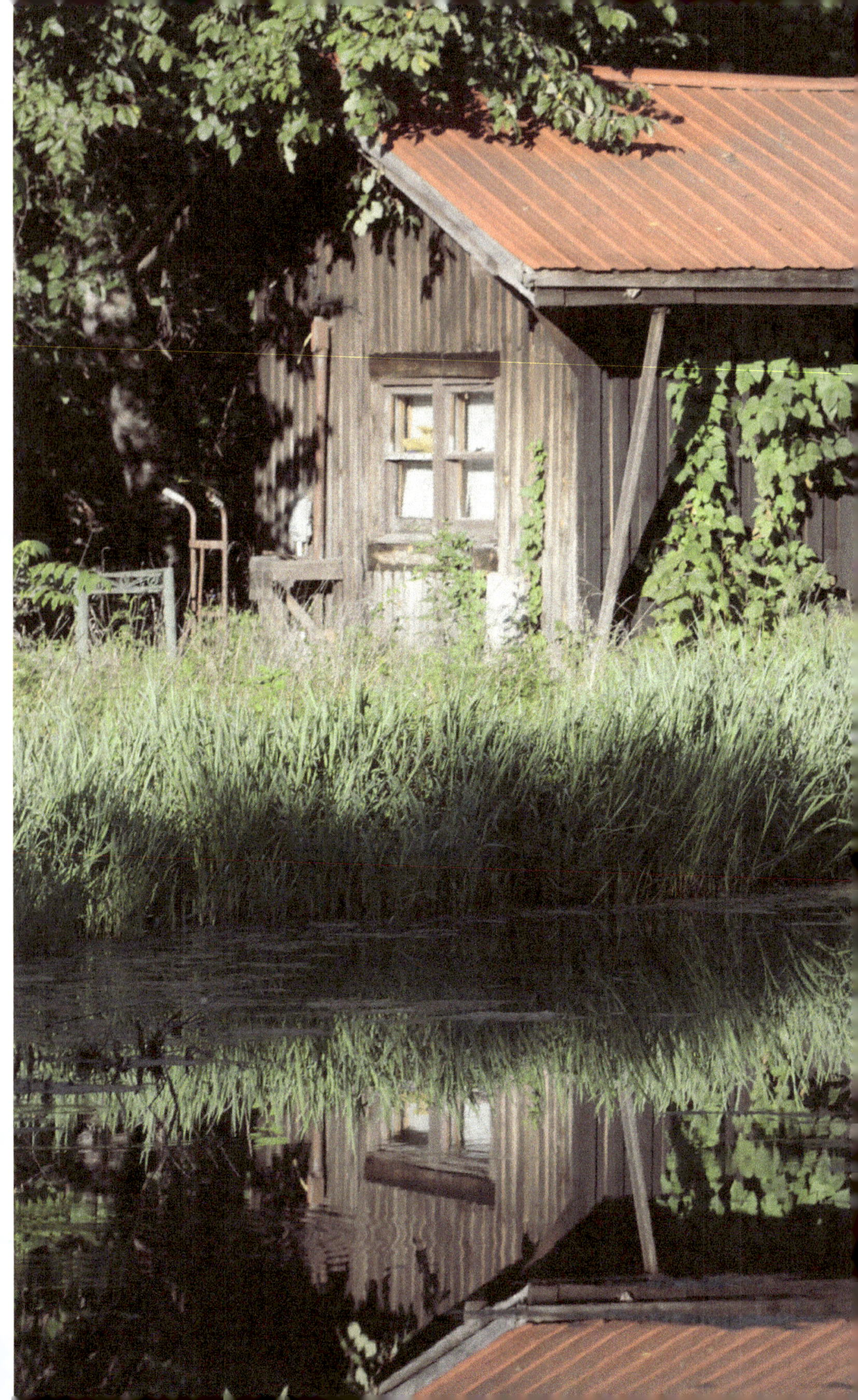

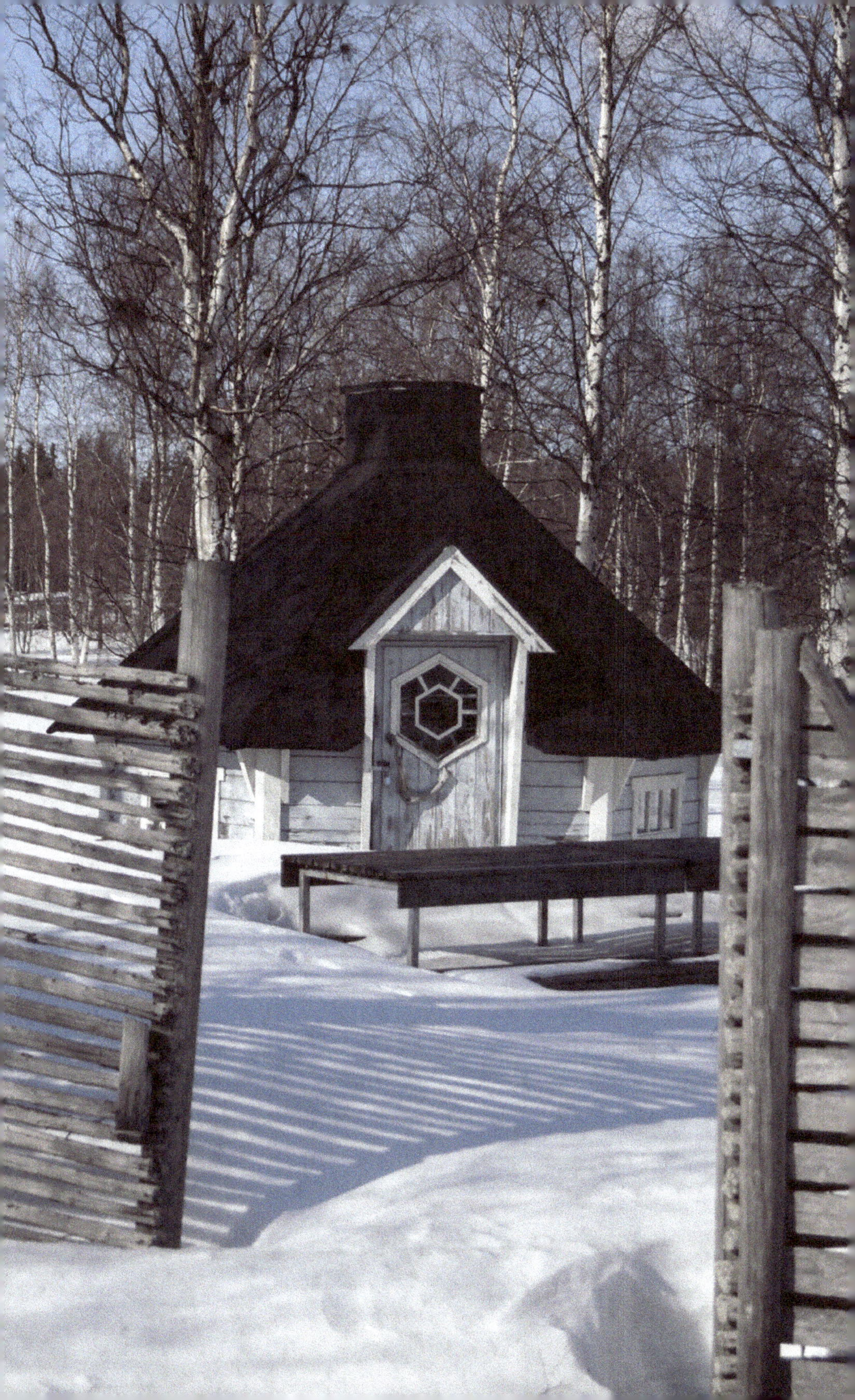

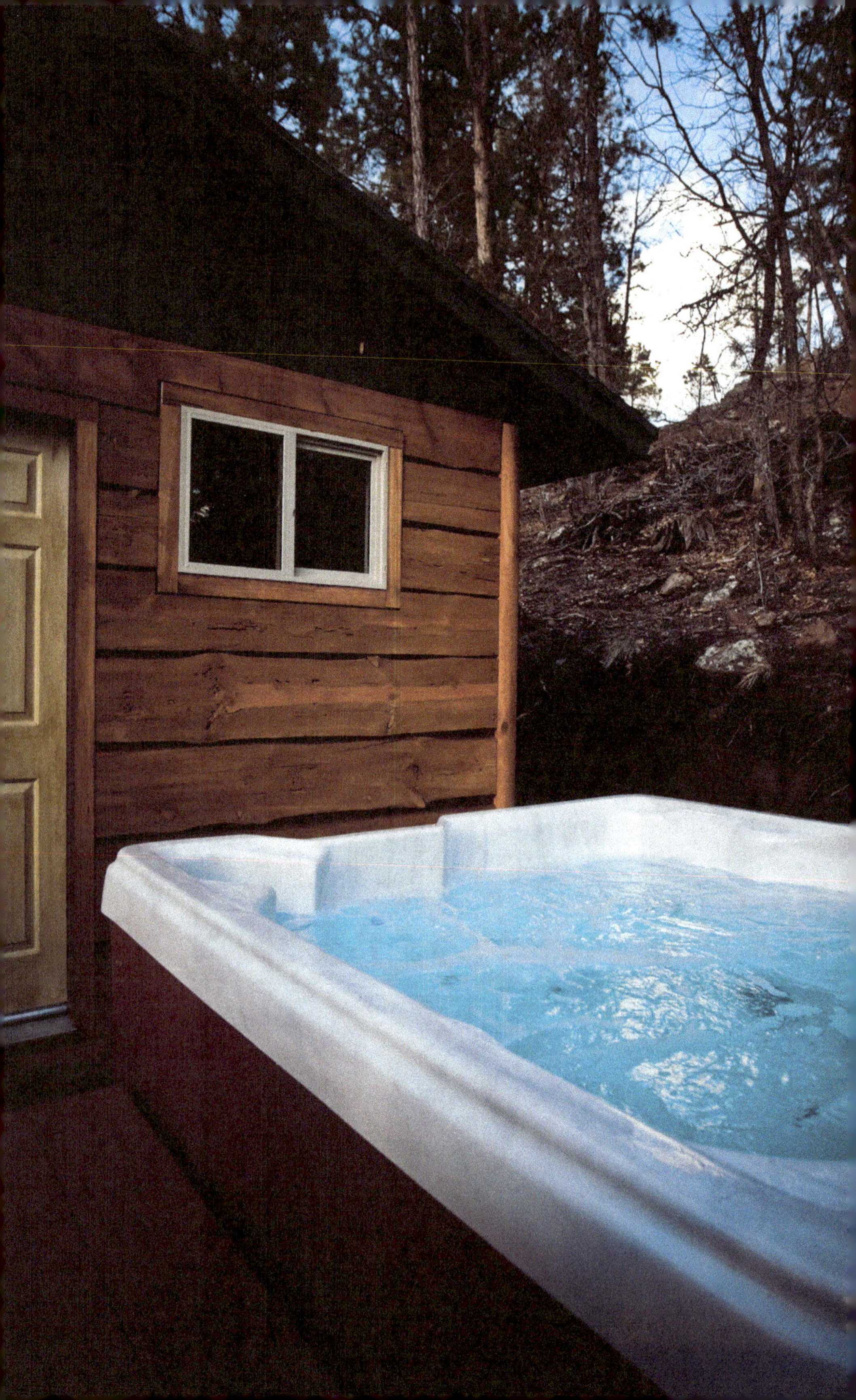

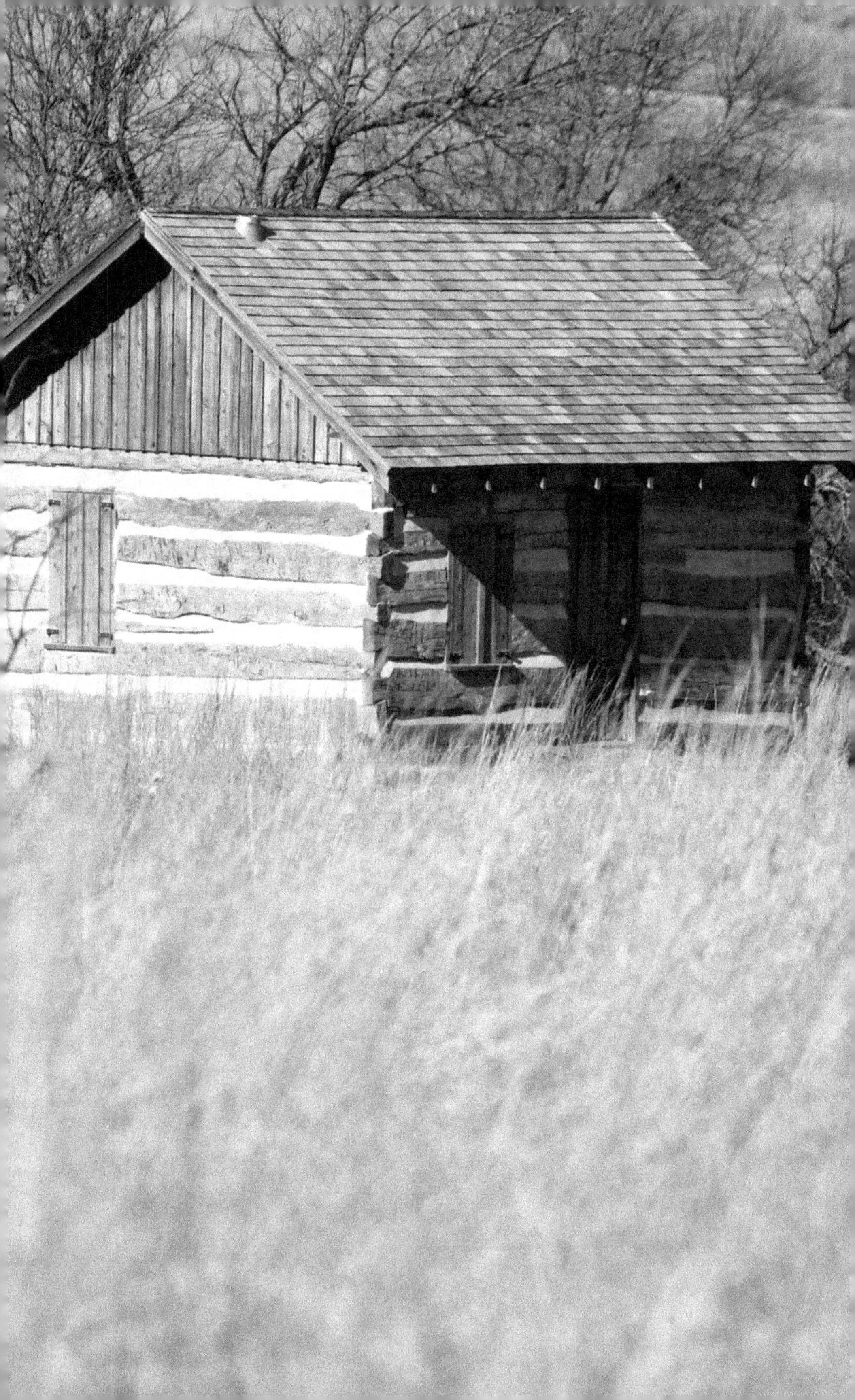

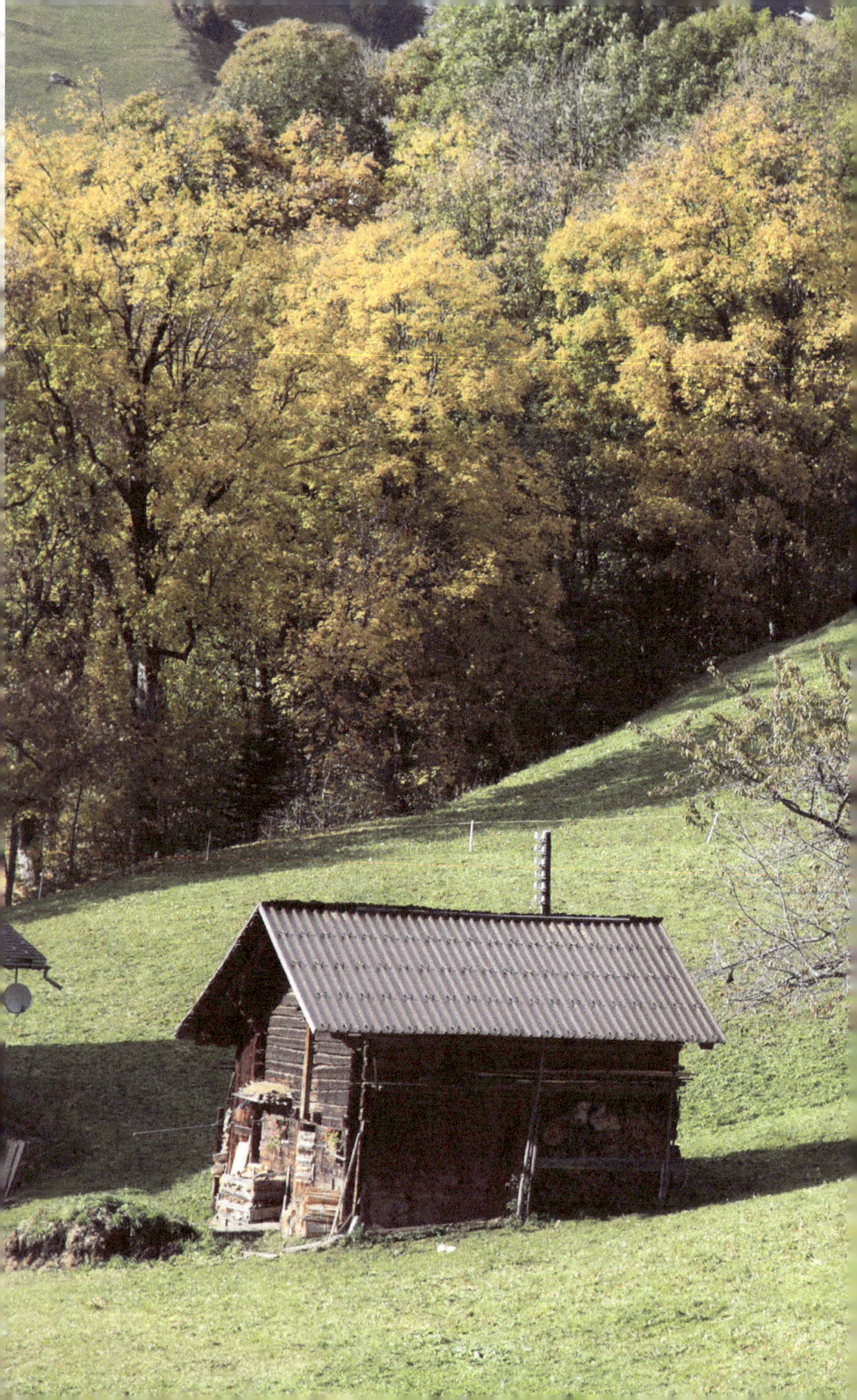

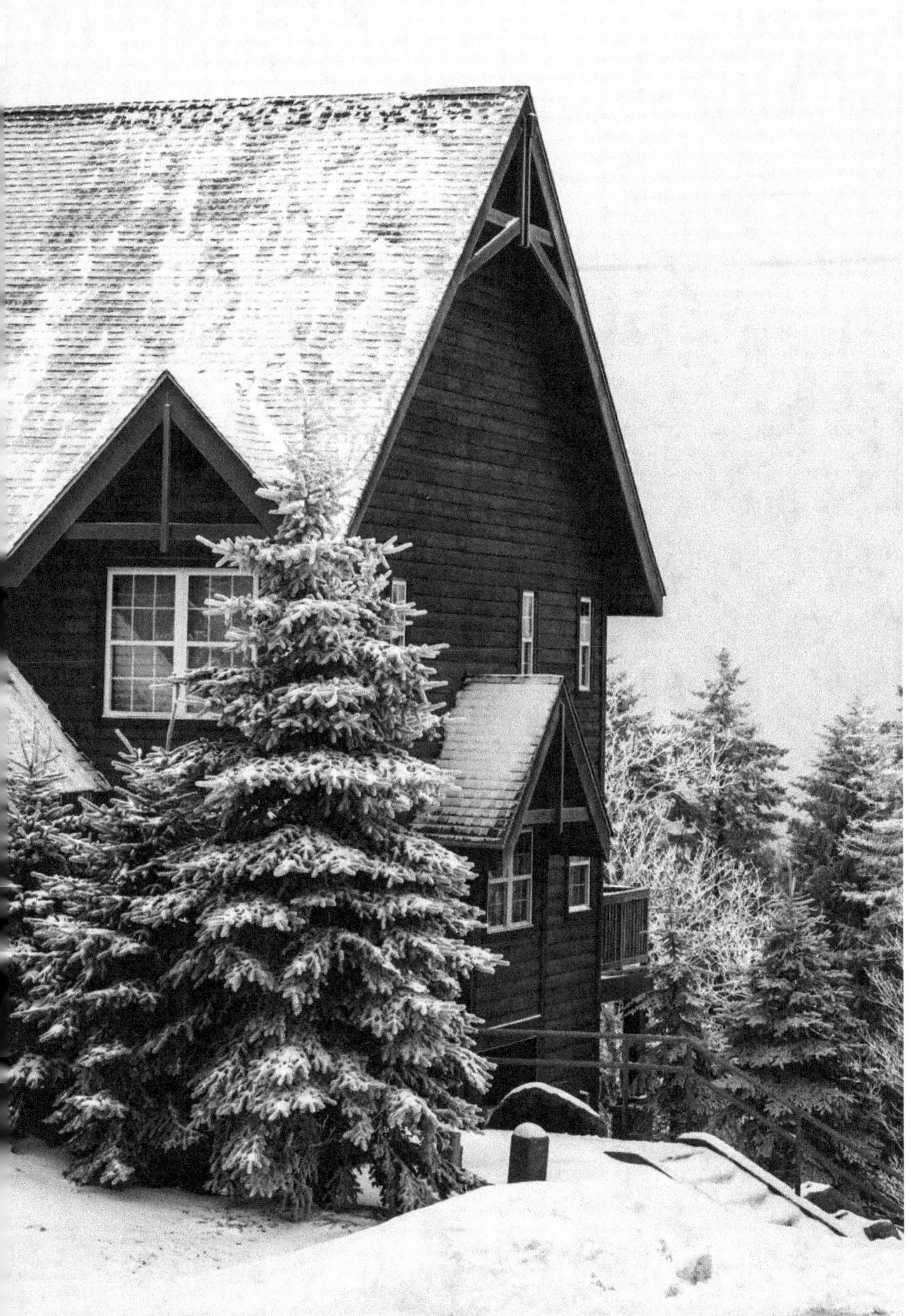

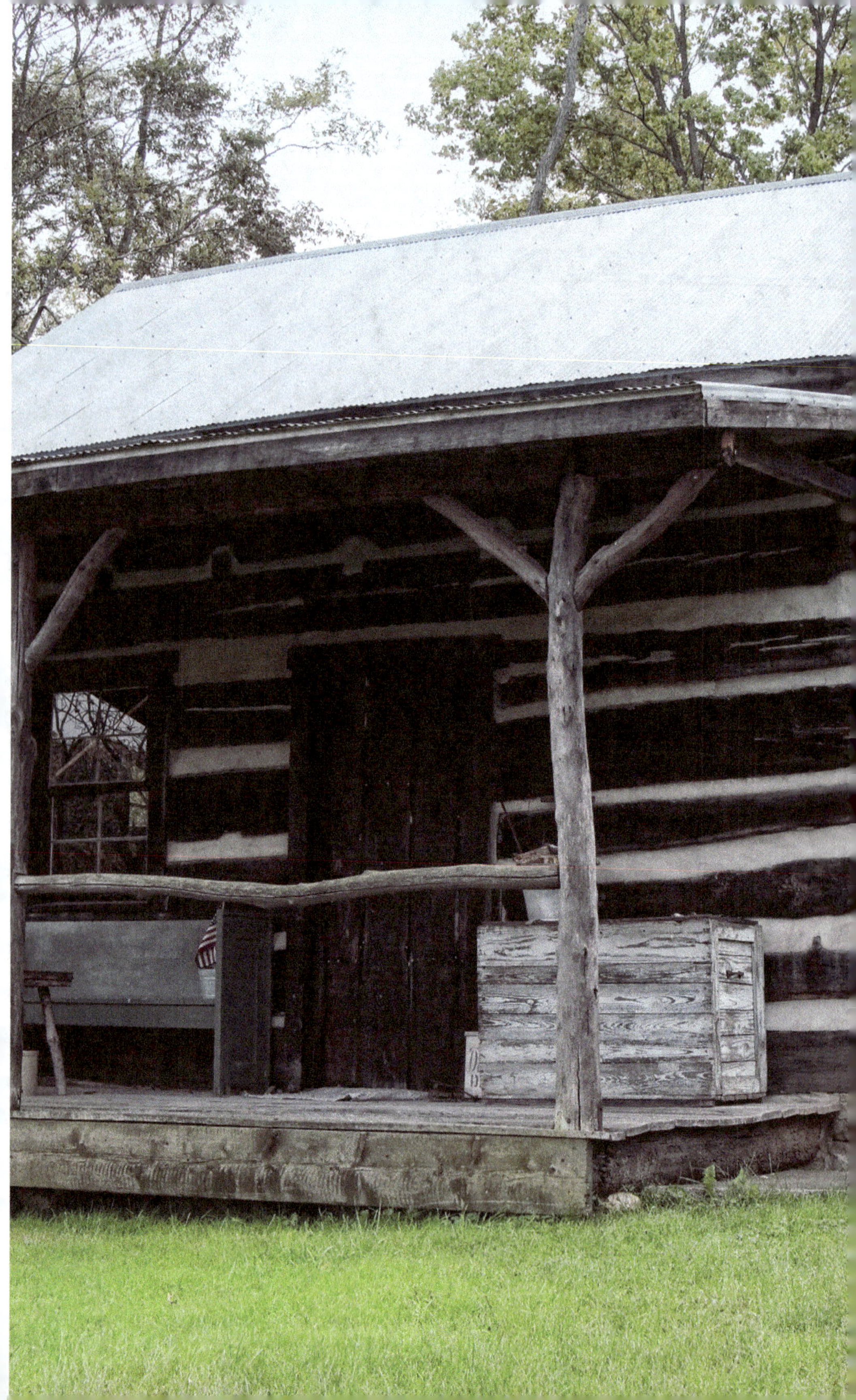

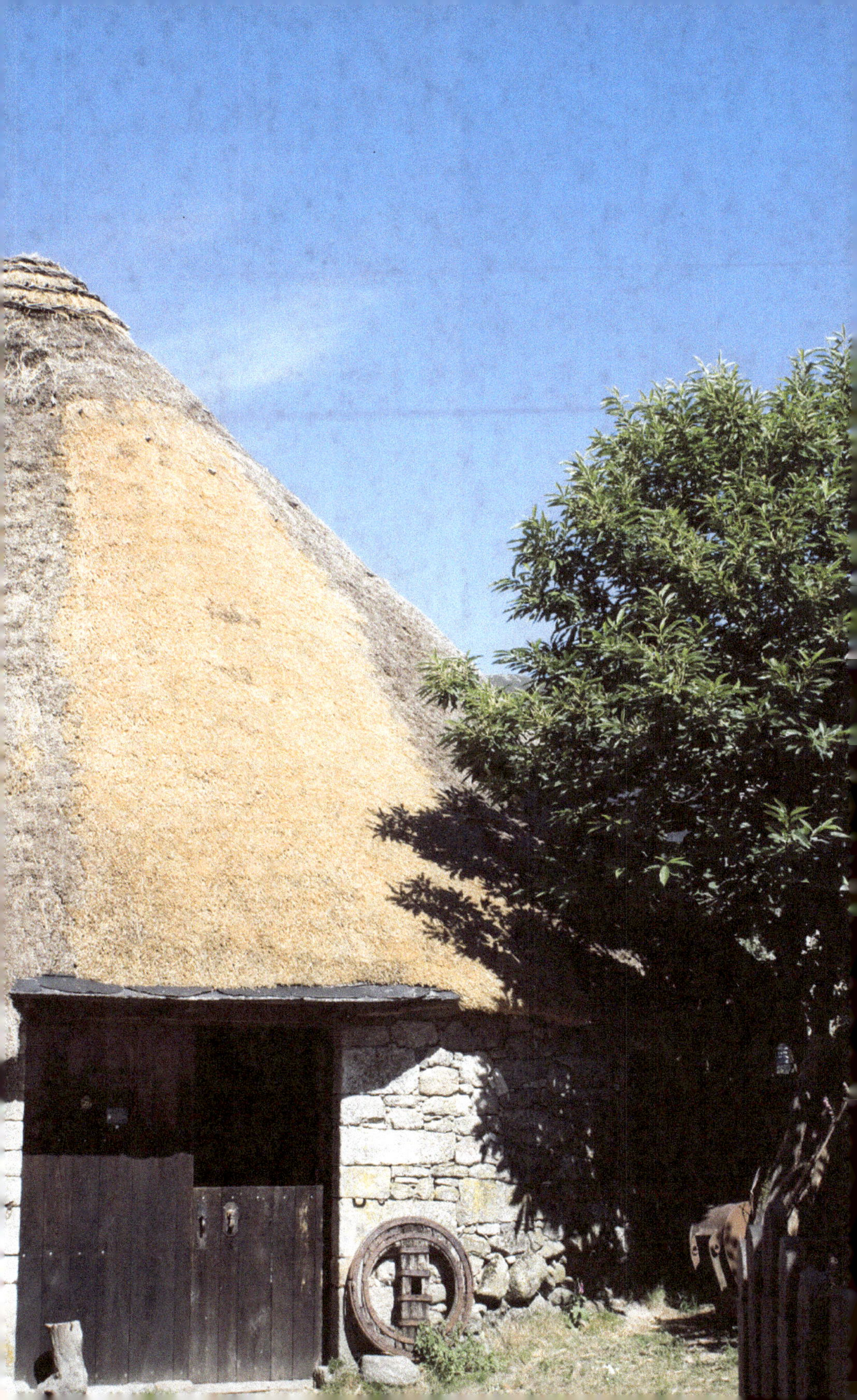

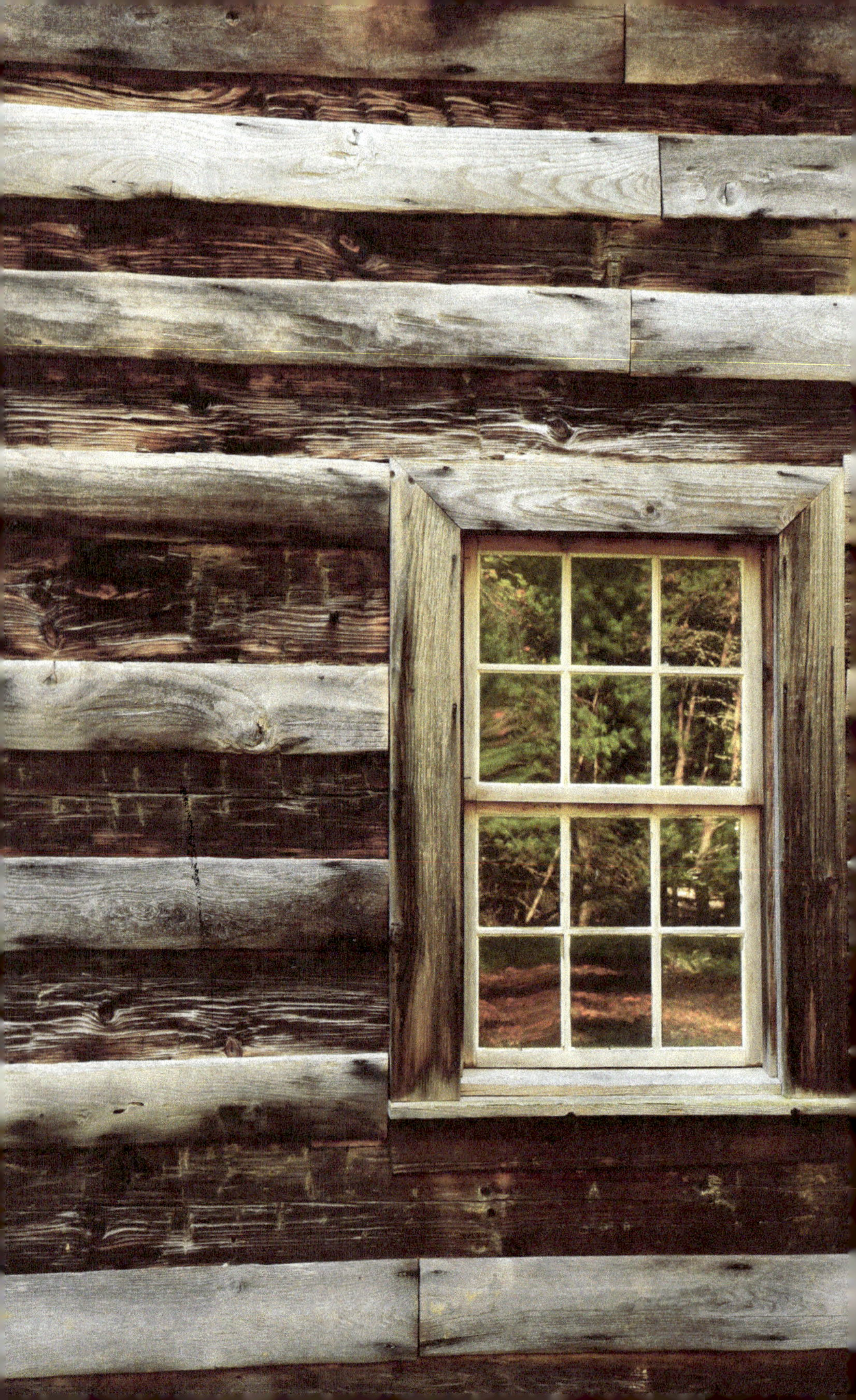

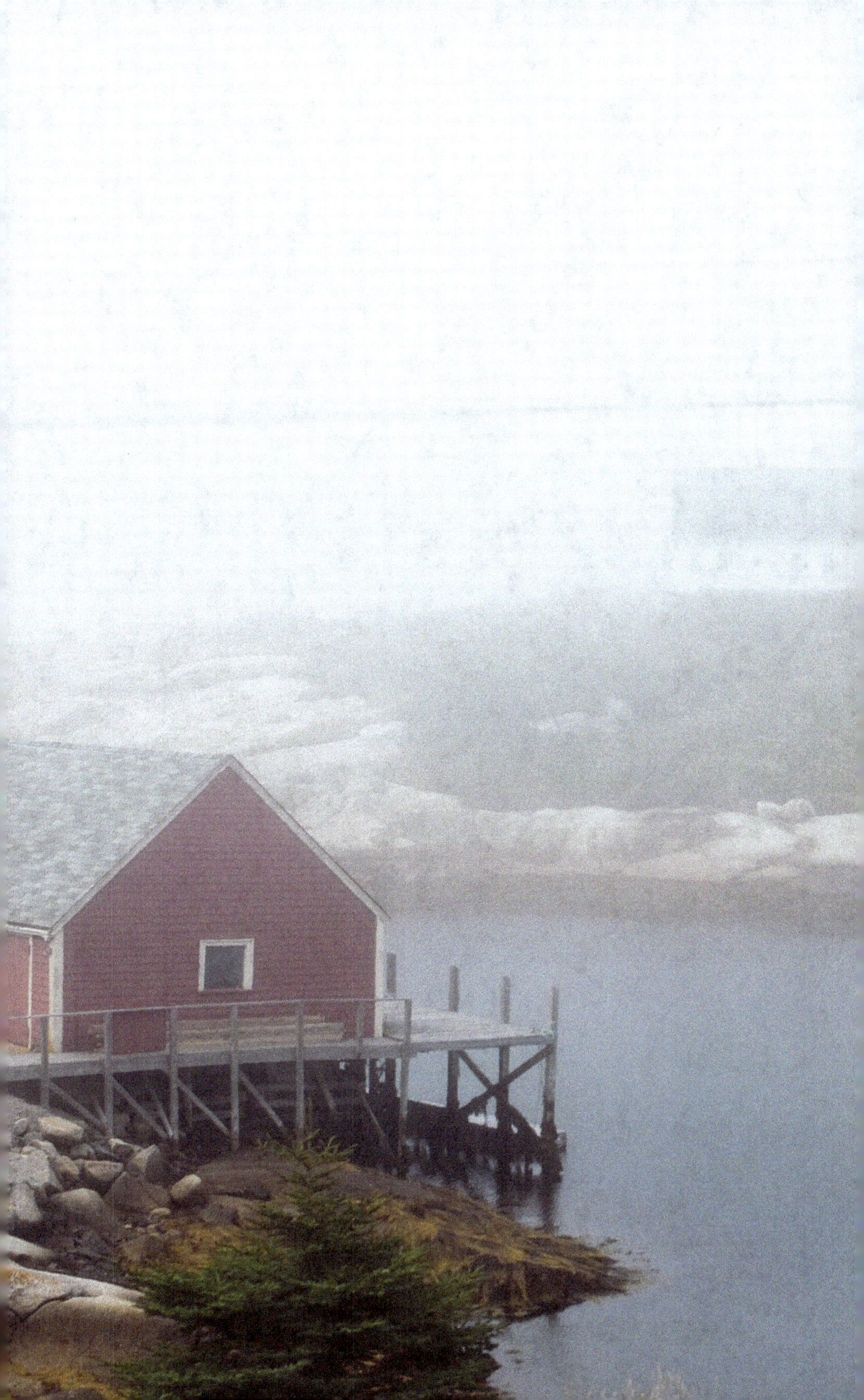

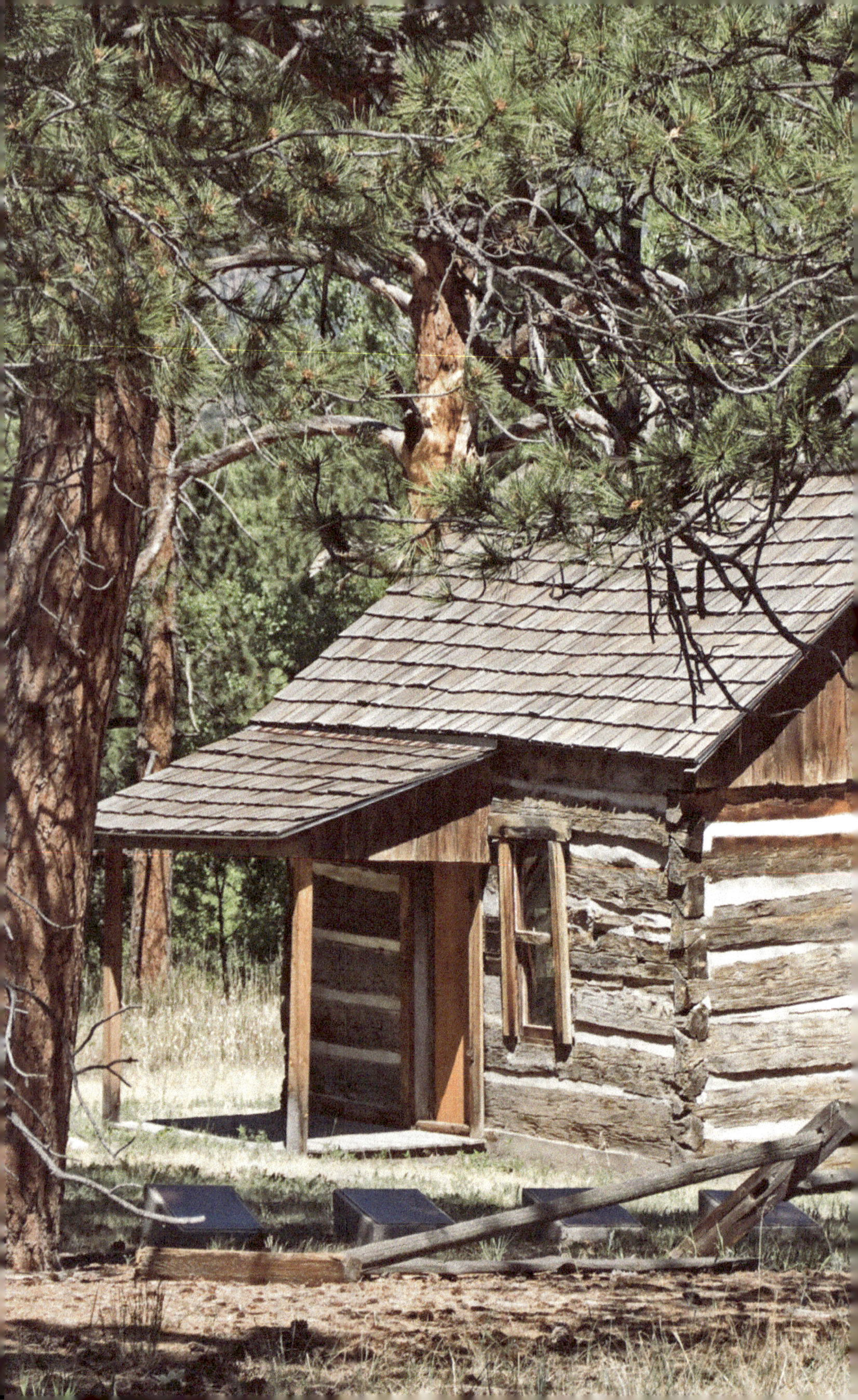

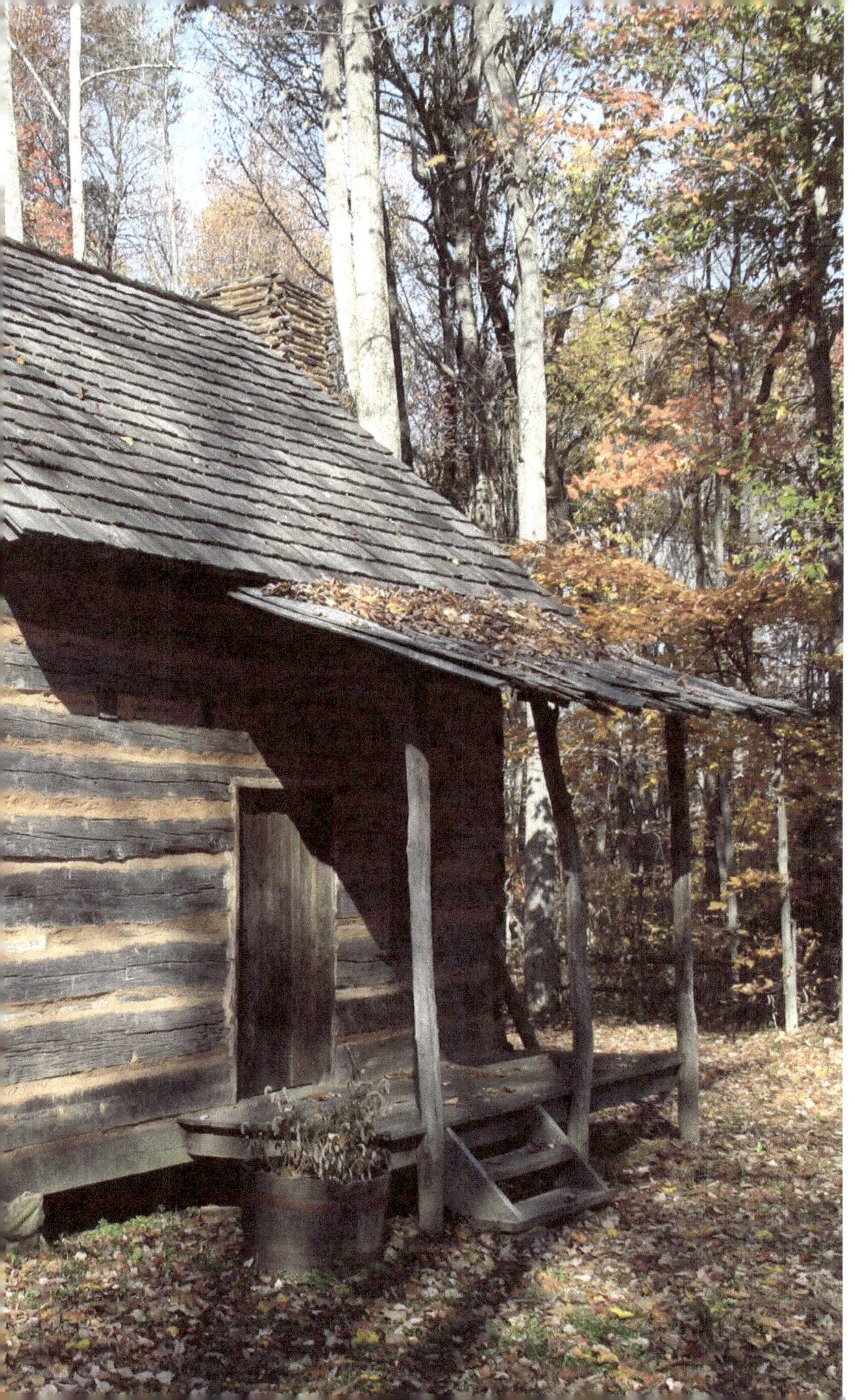

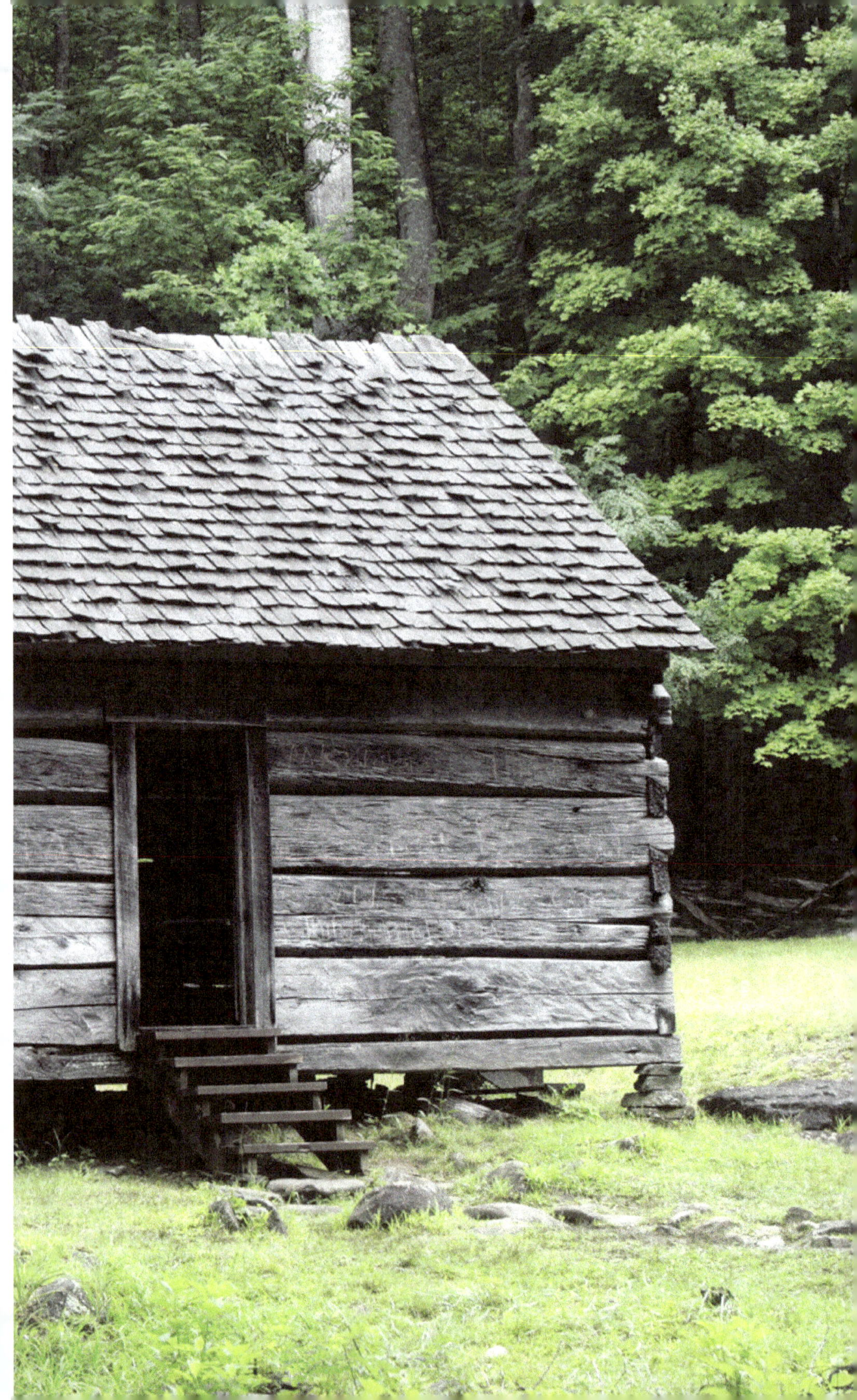

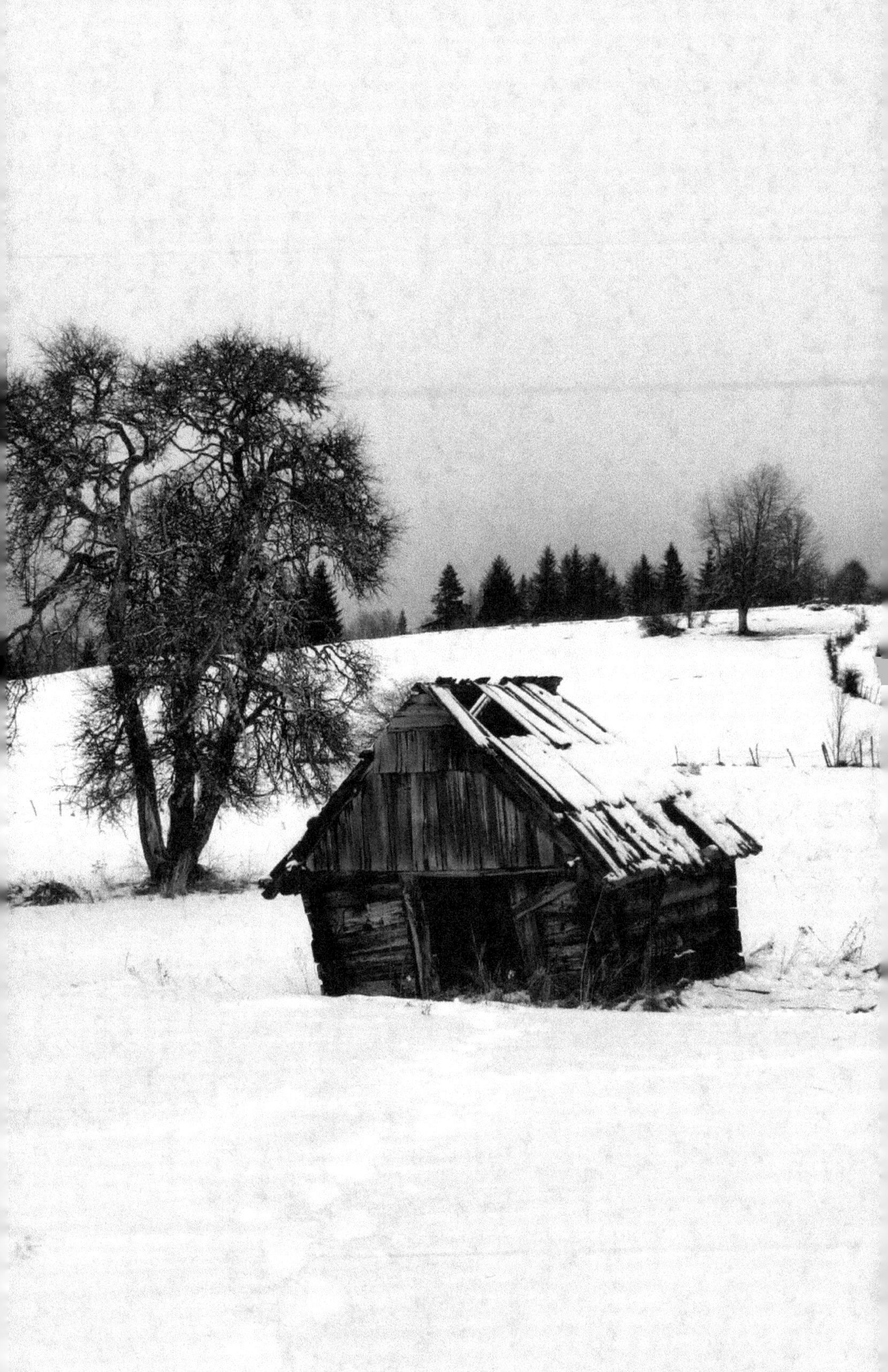

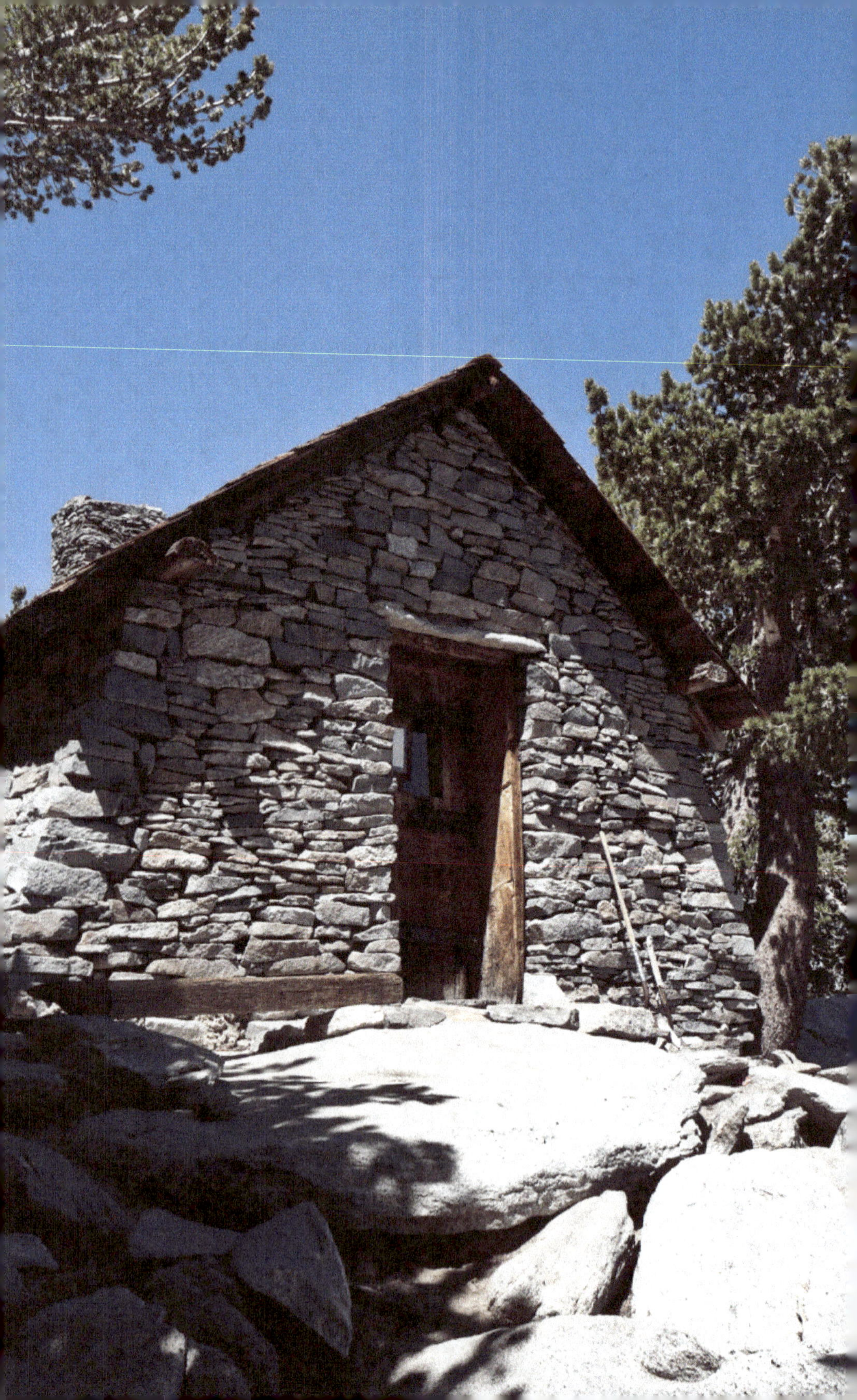

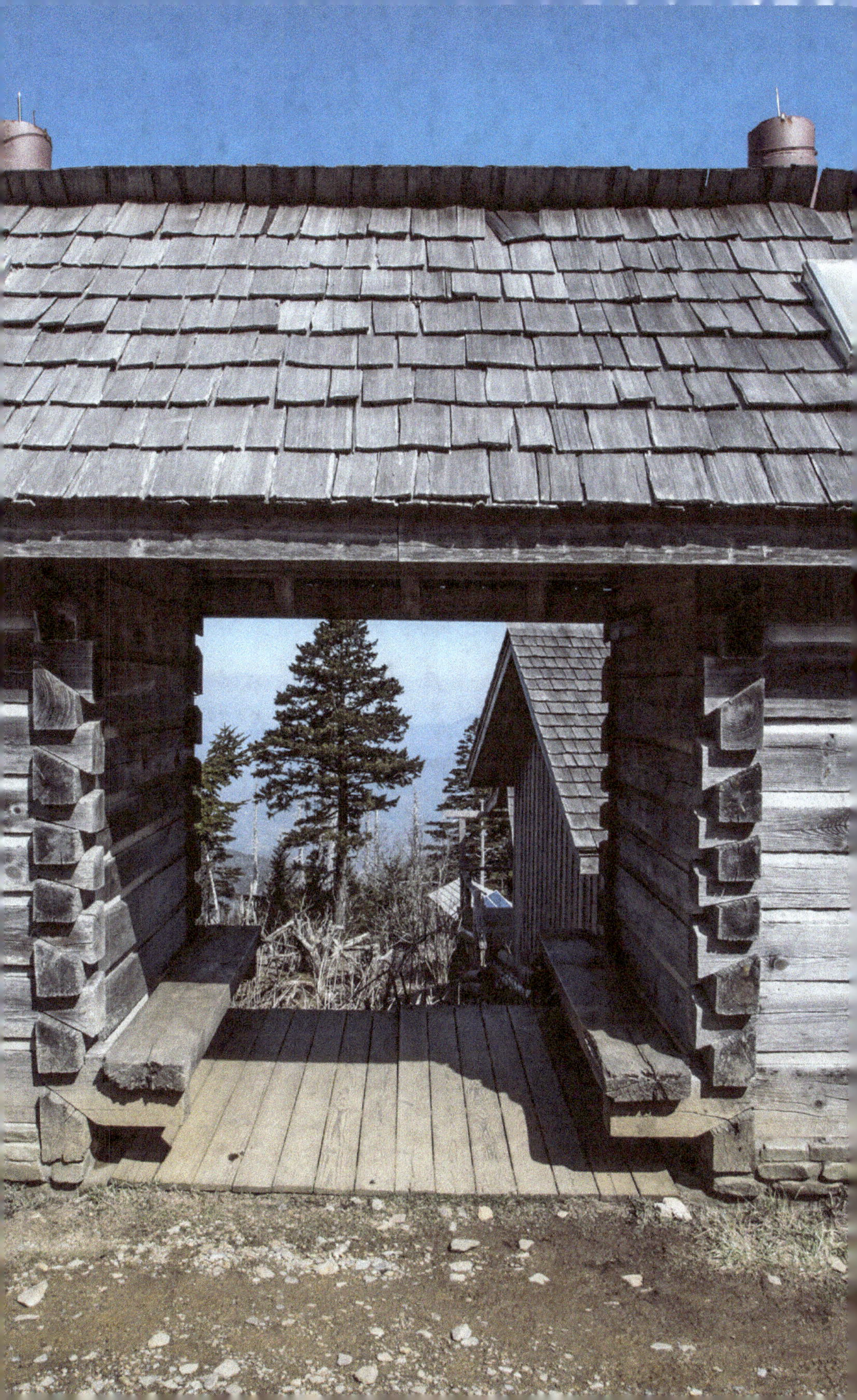

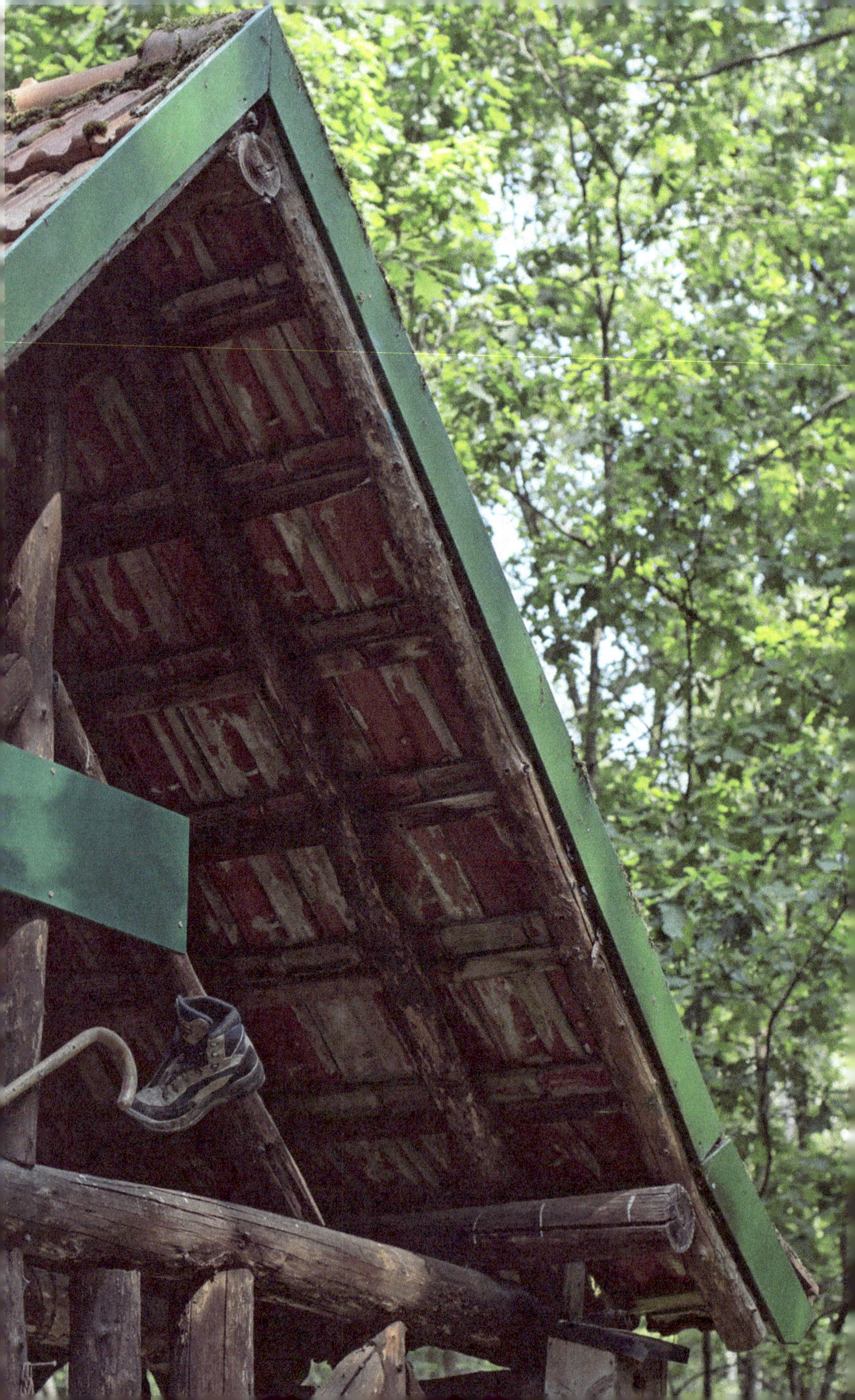

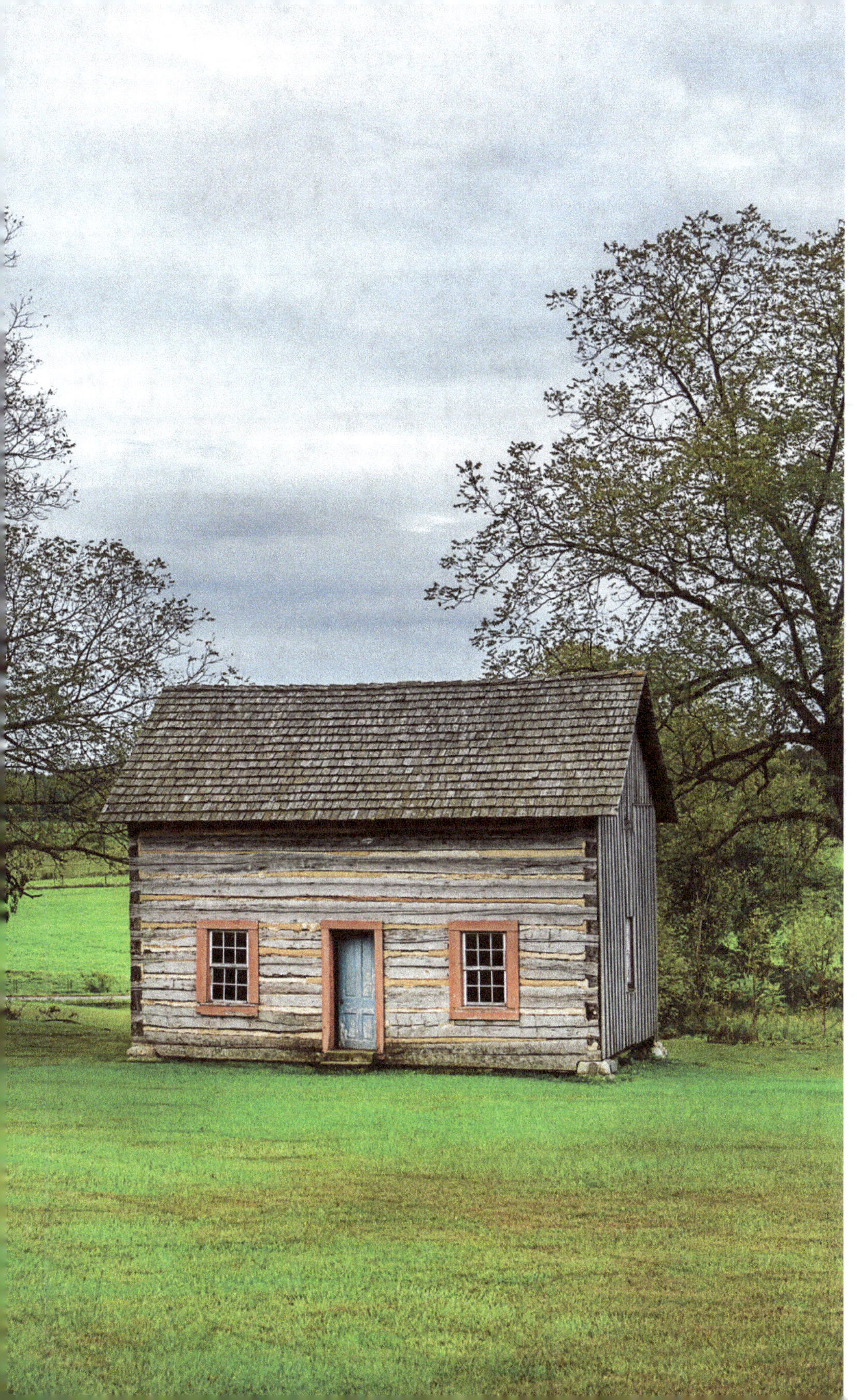

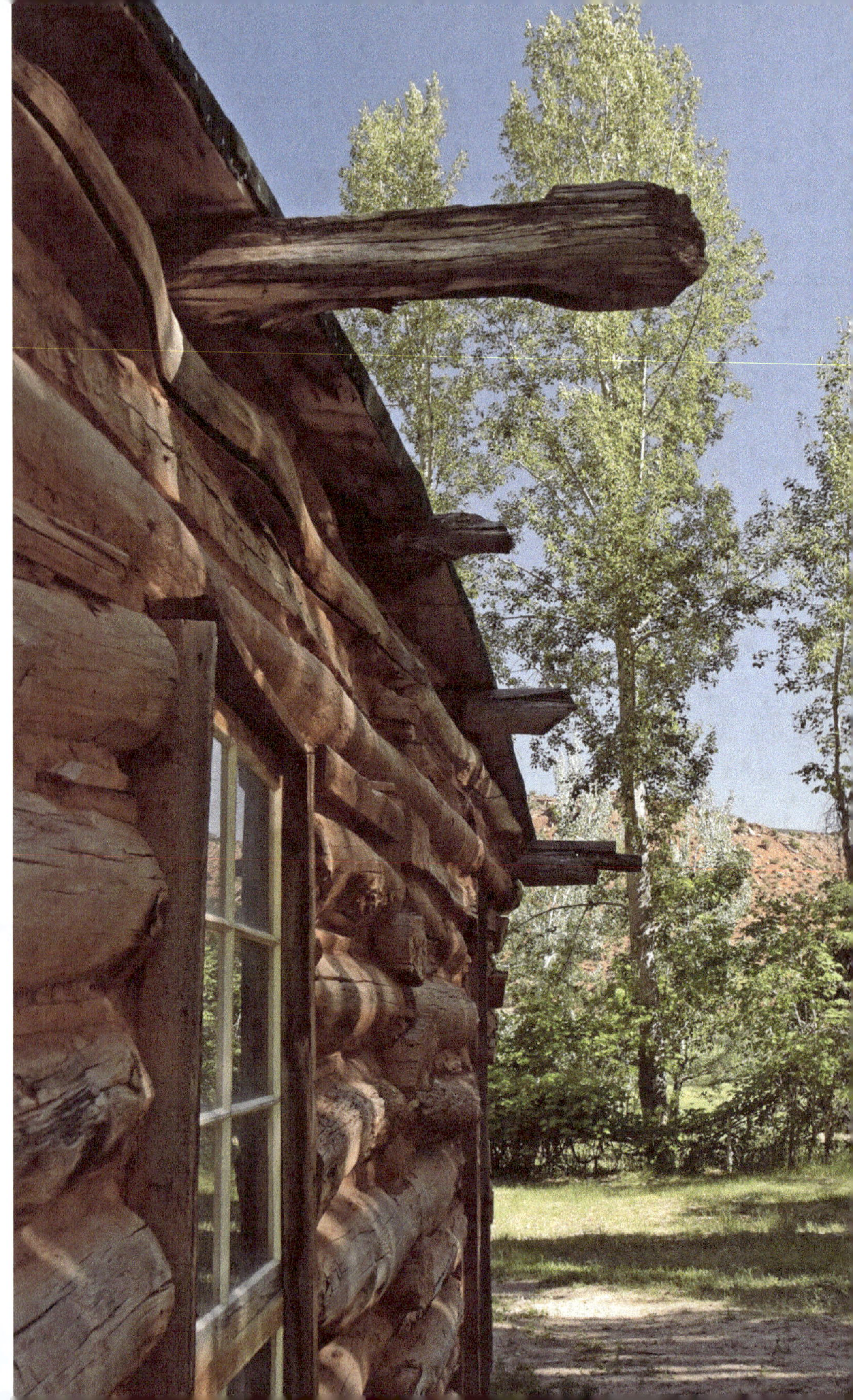

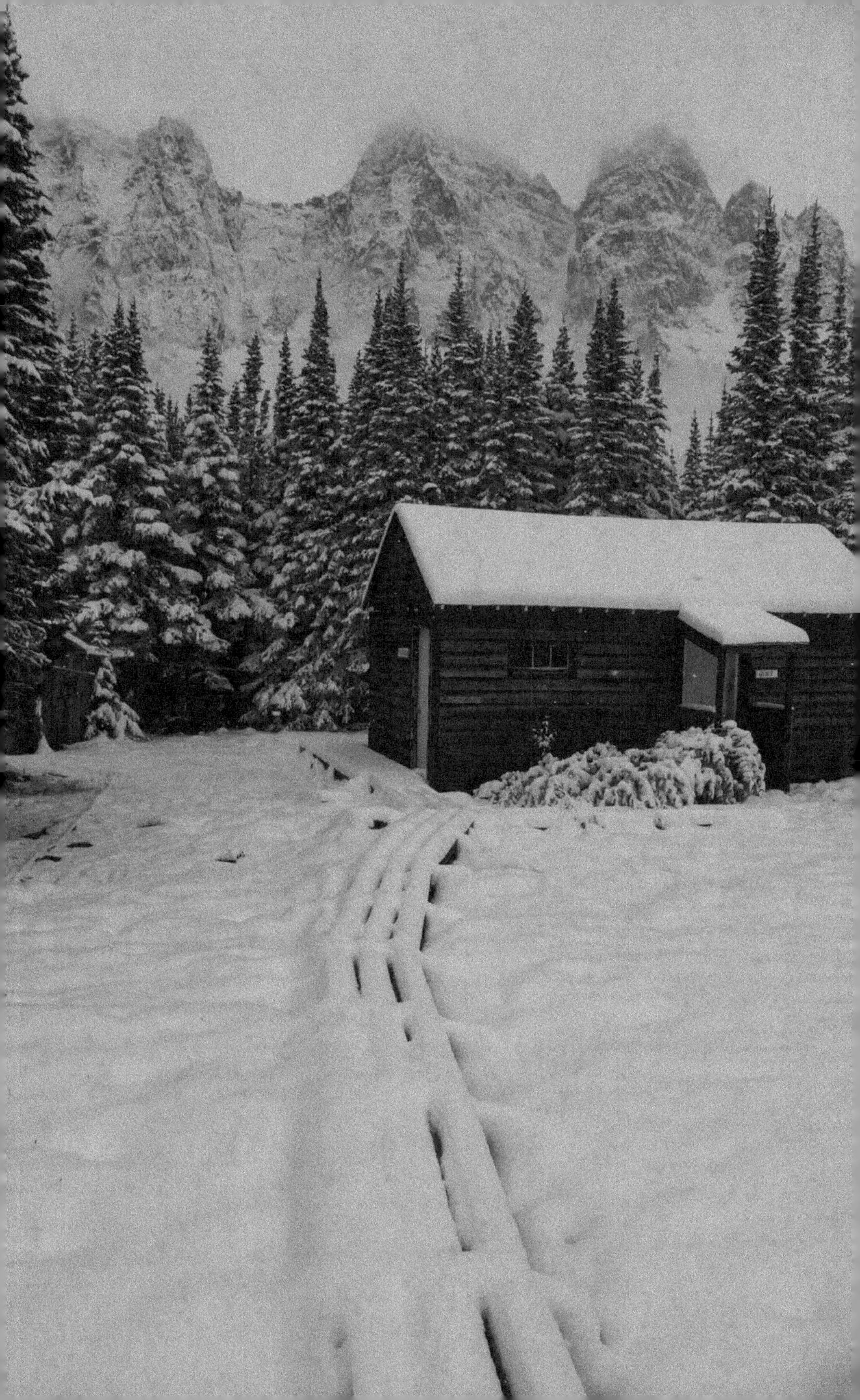

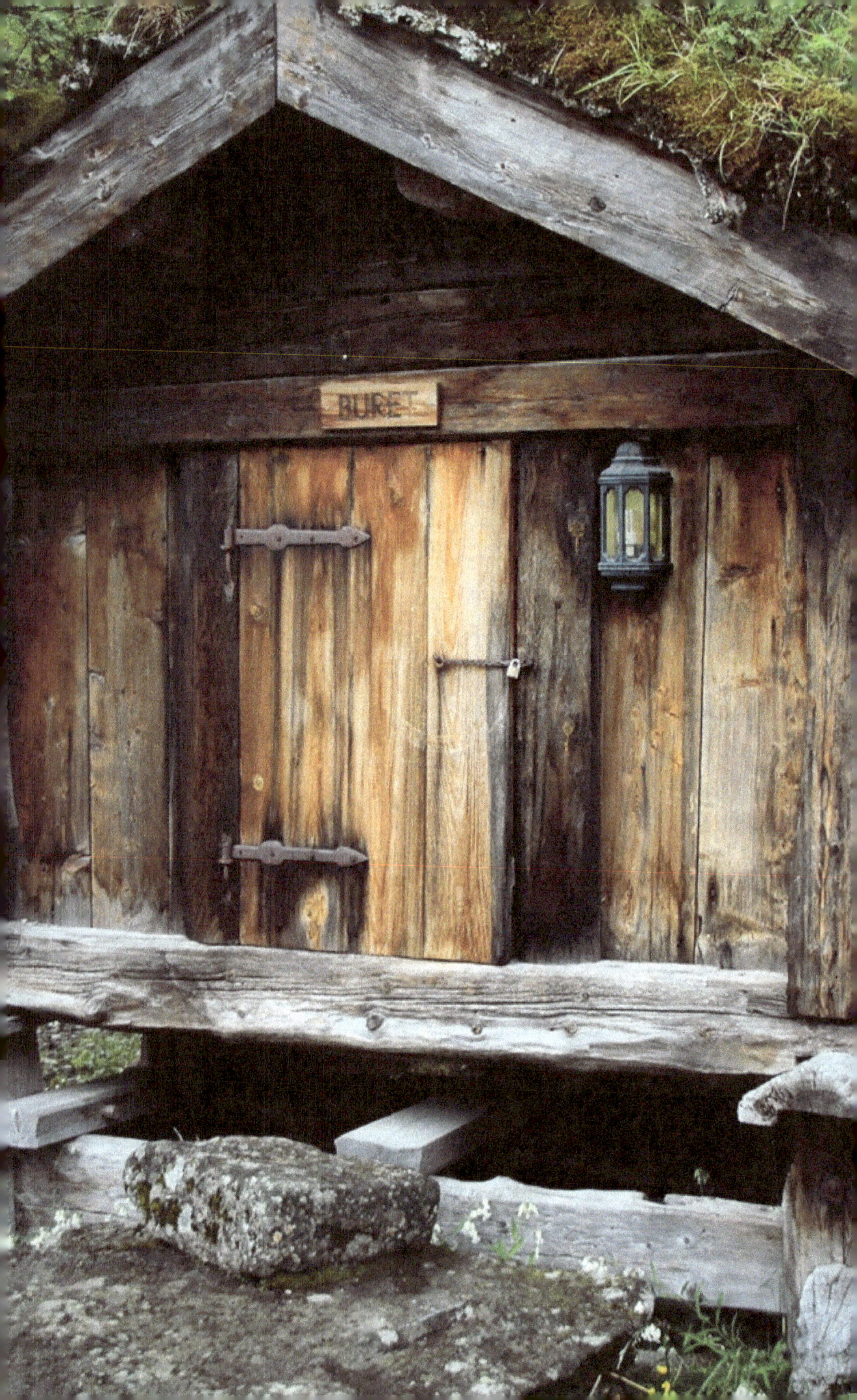
BURET

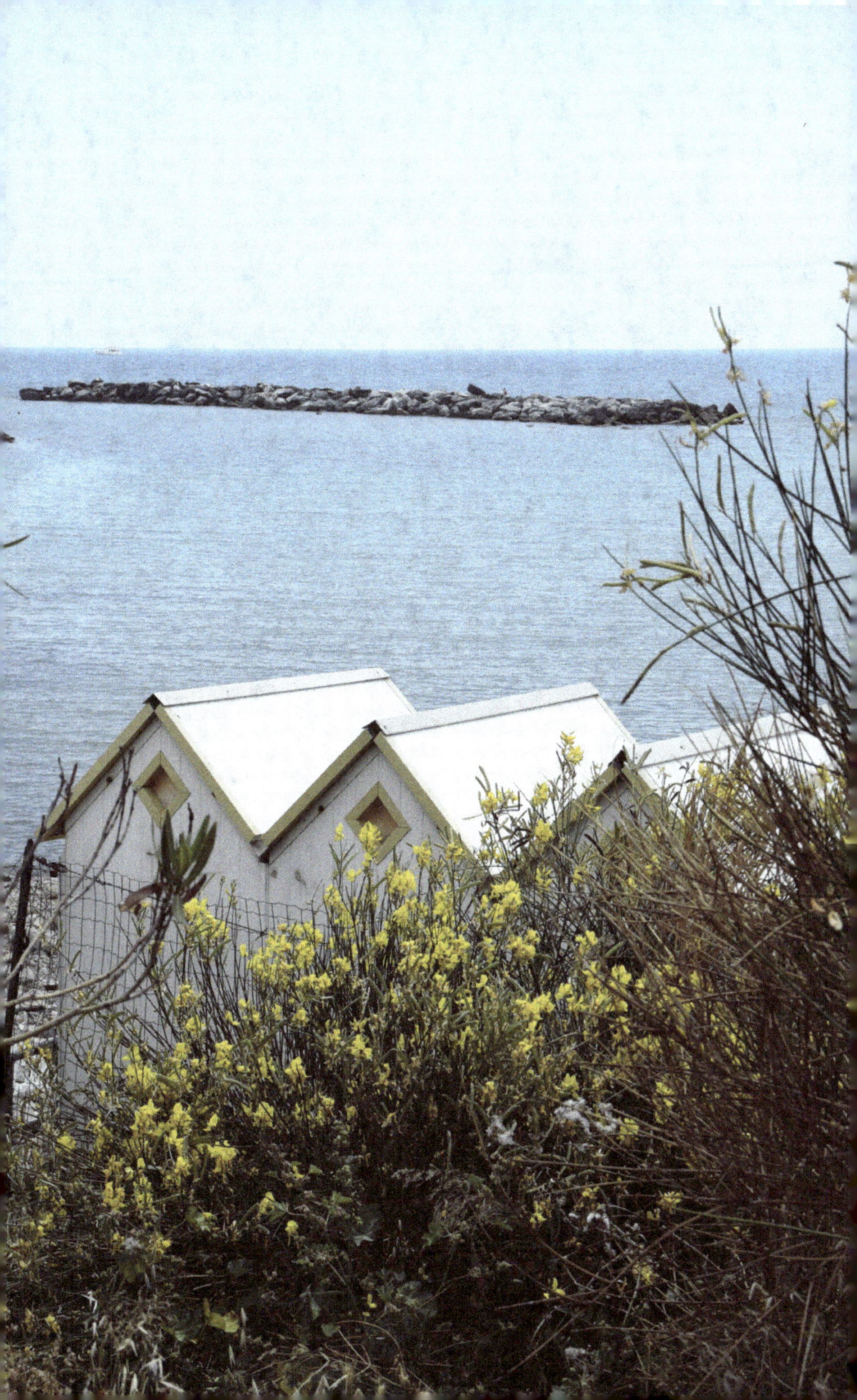

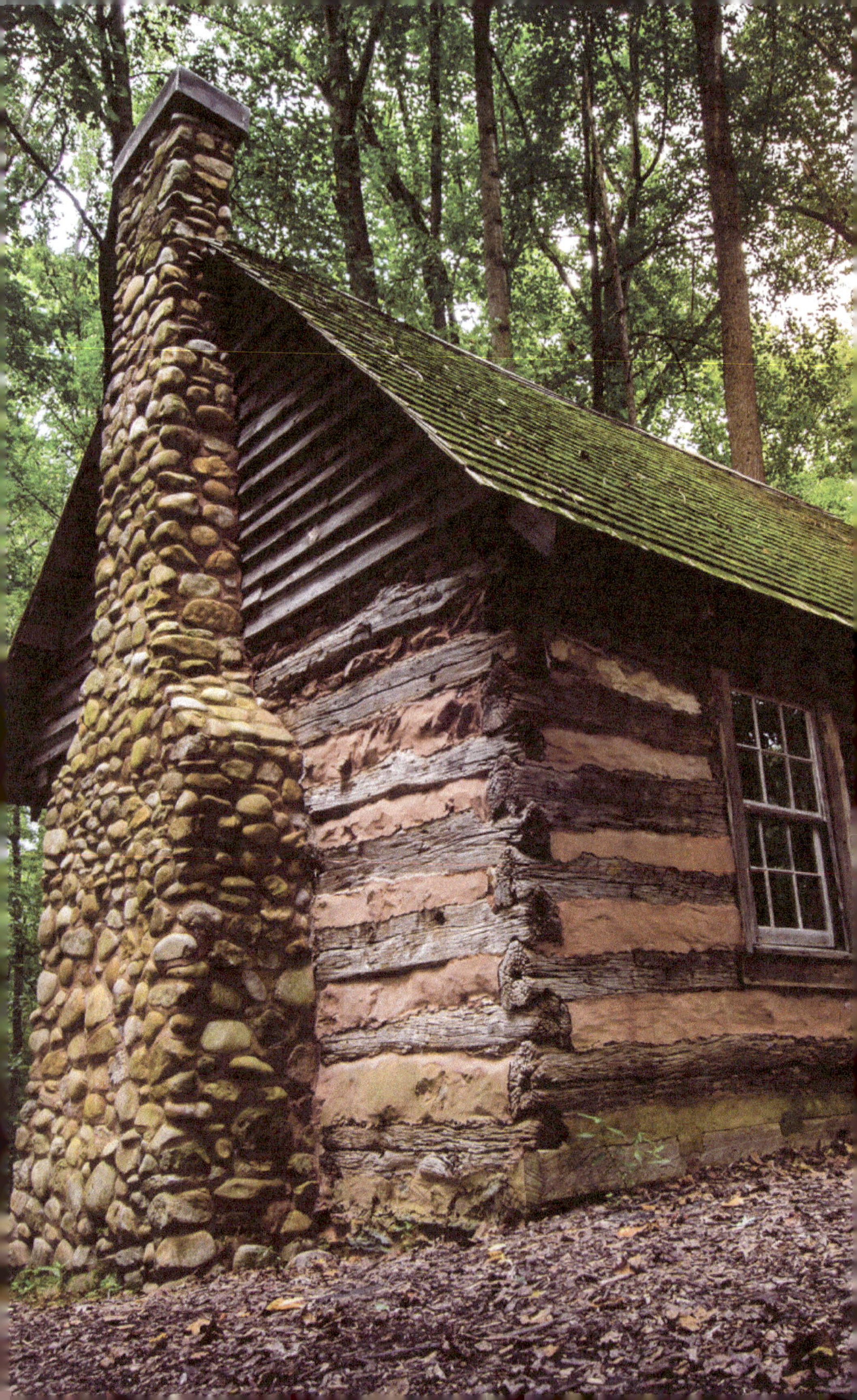

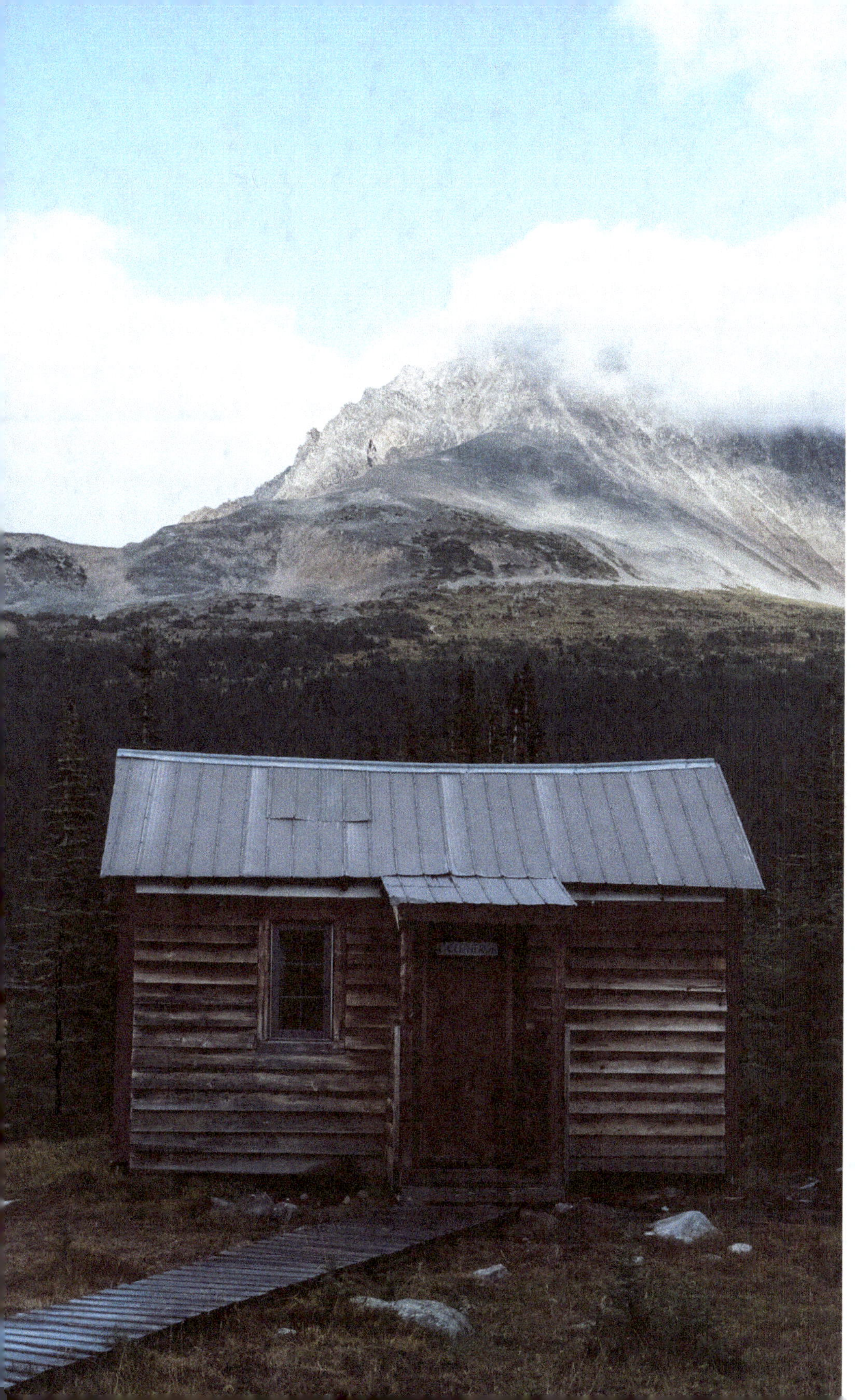

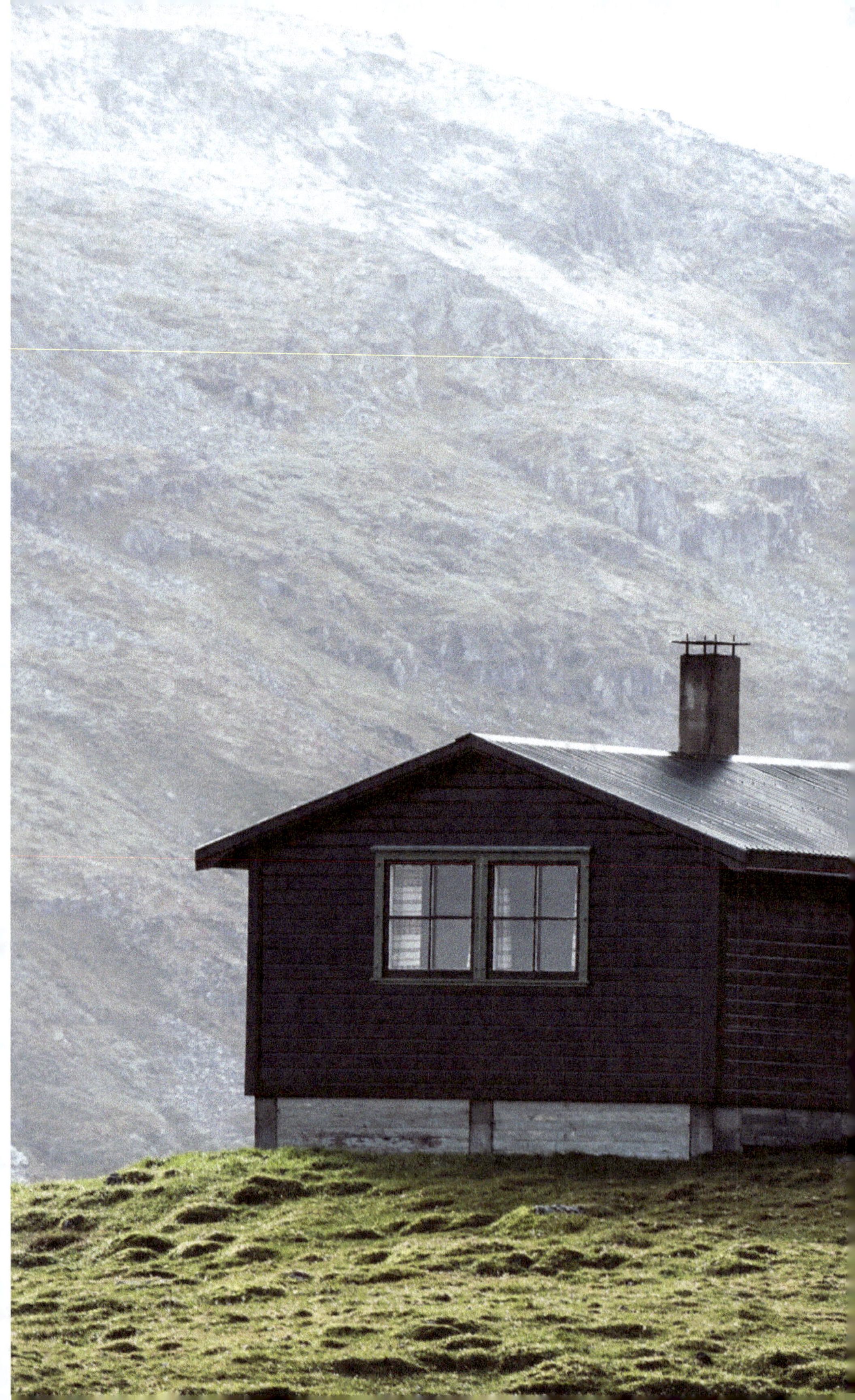

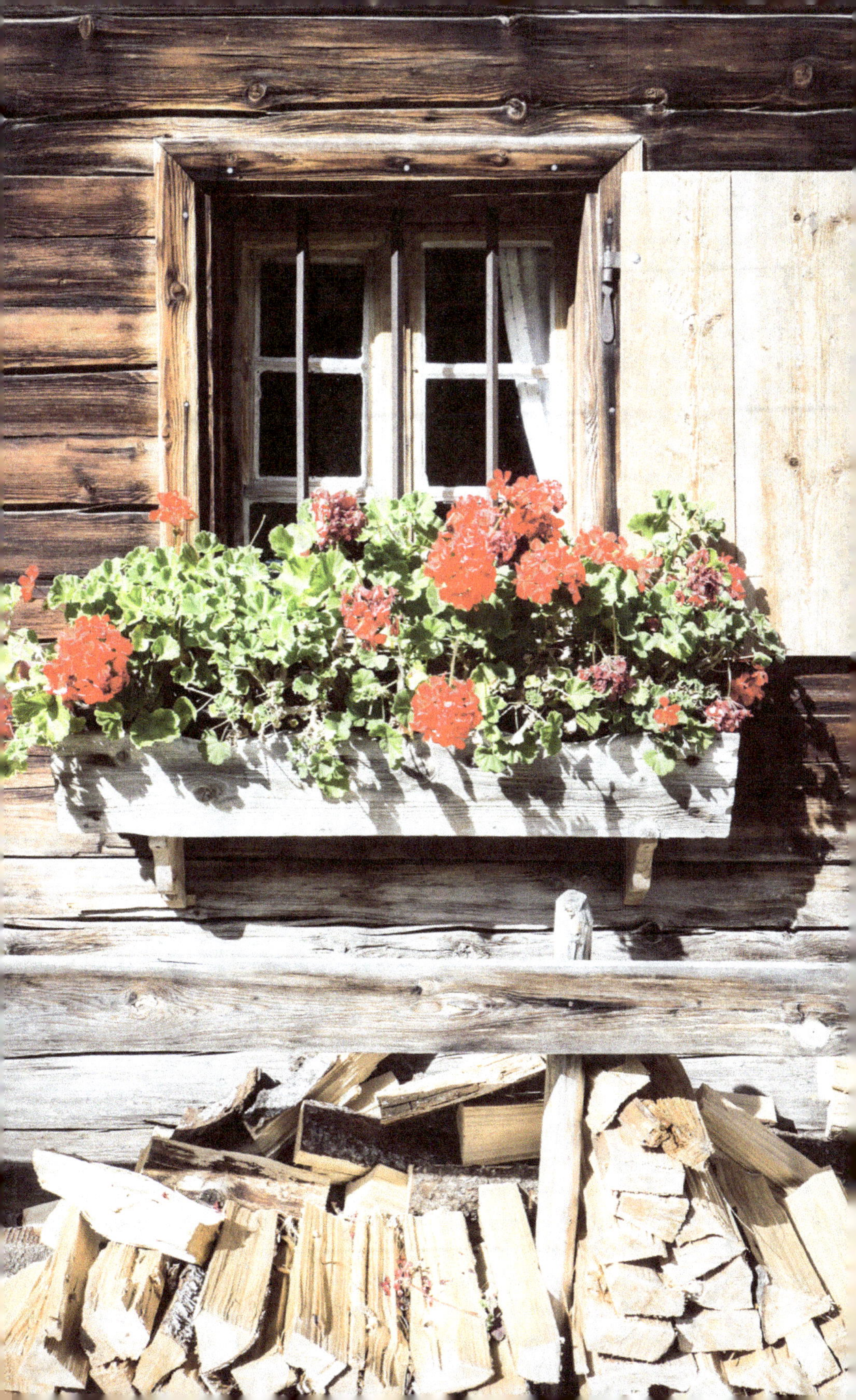

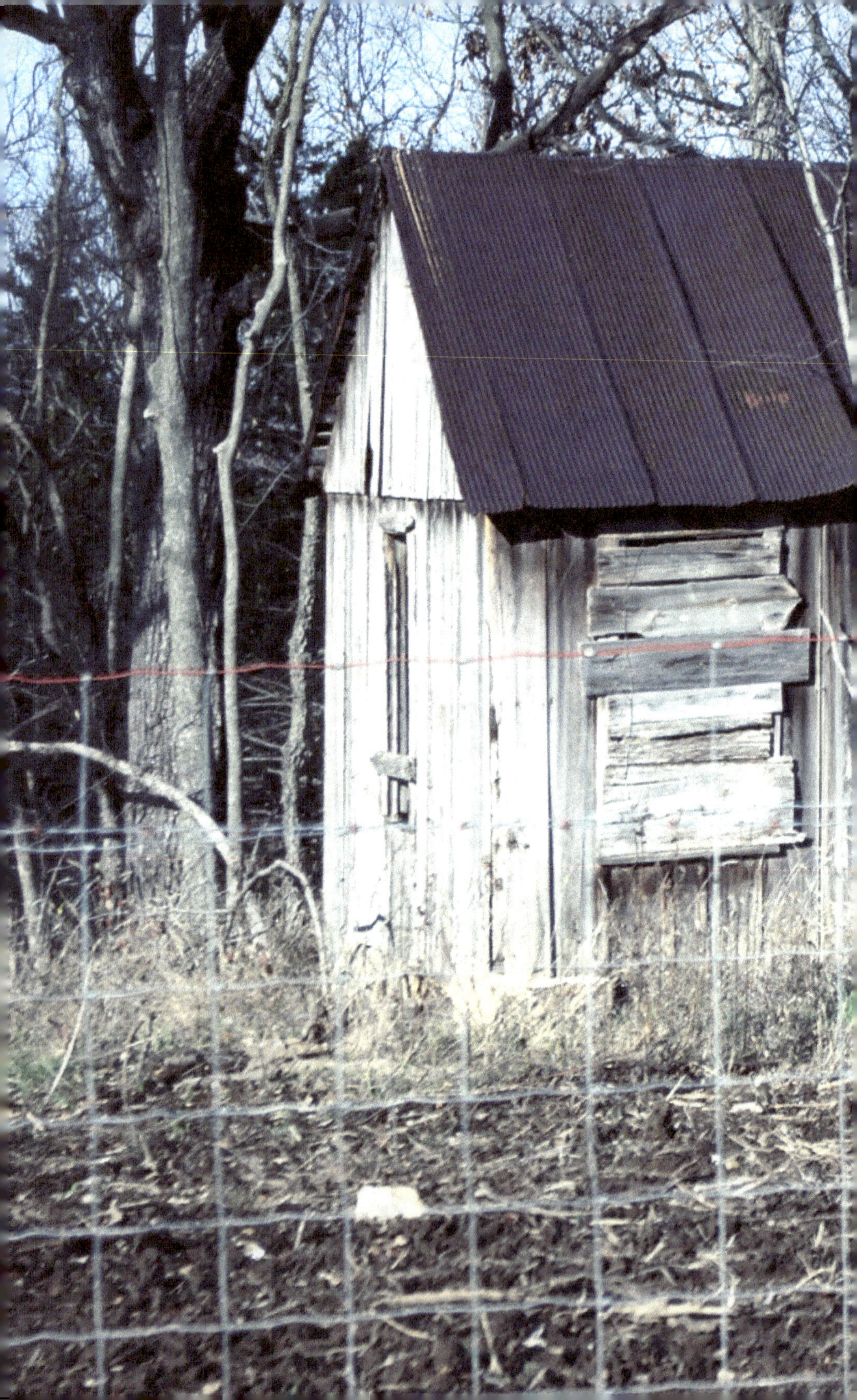

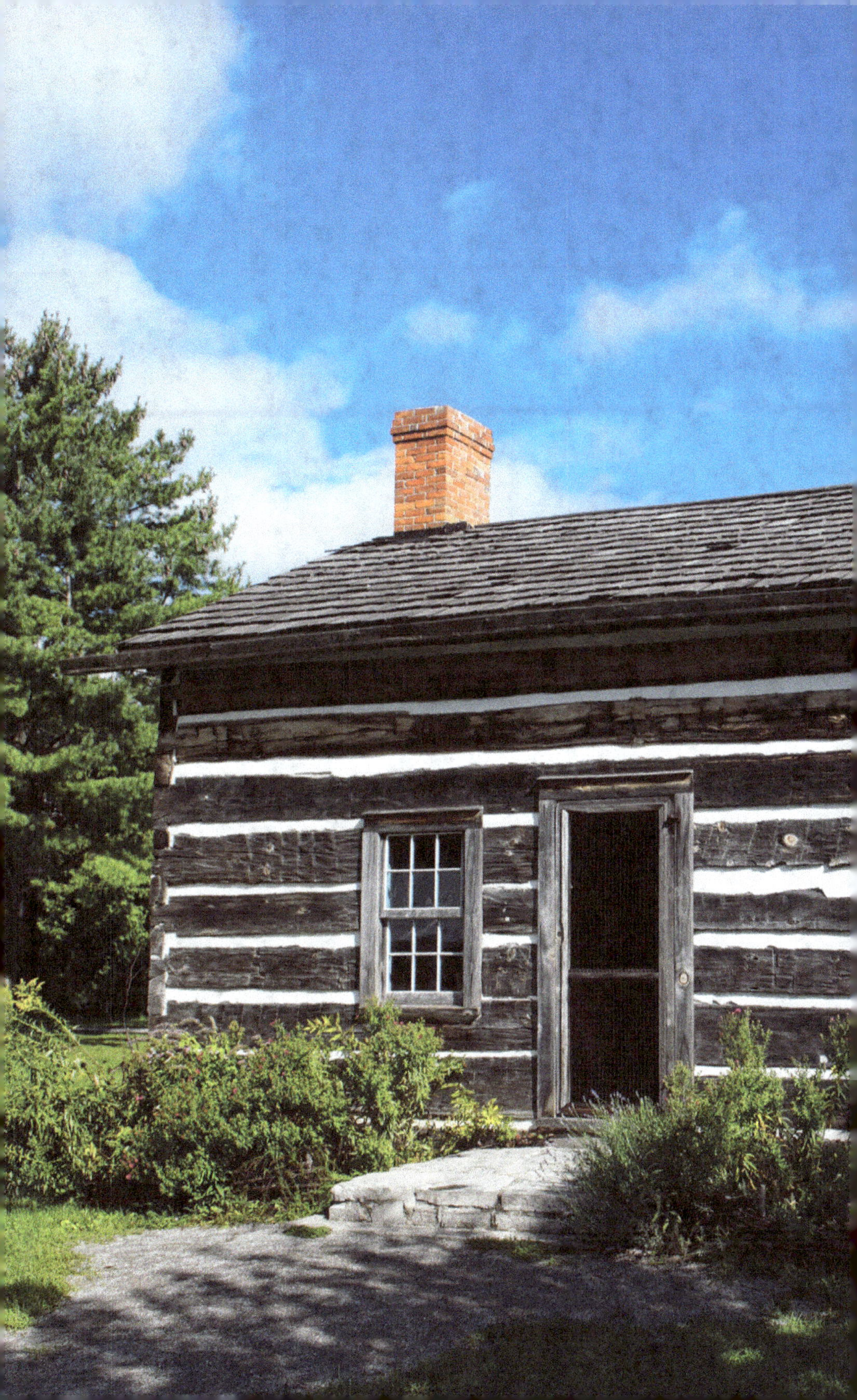

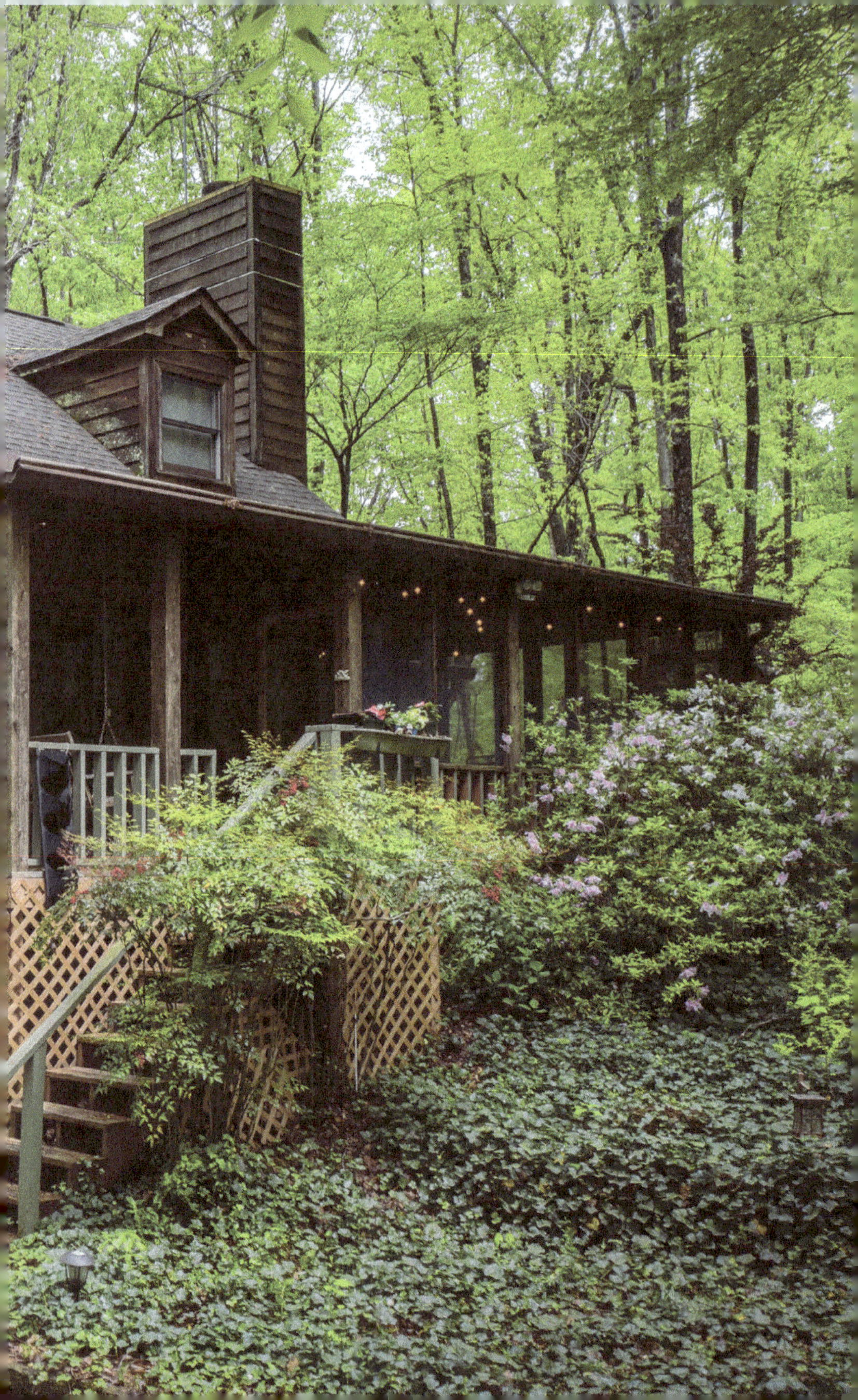

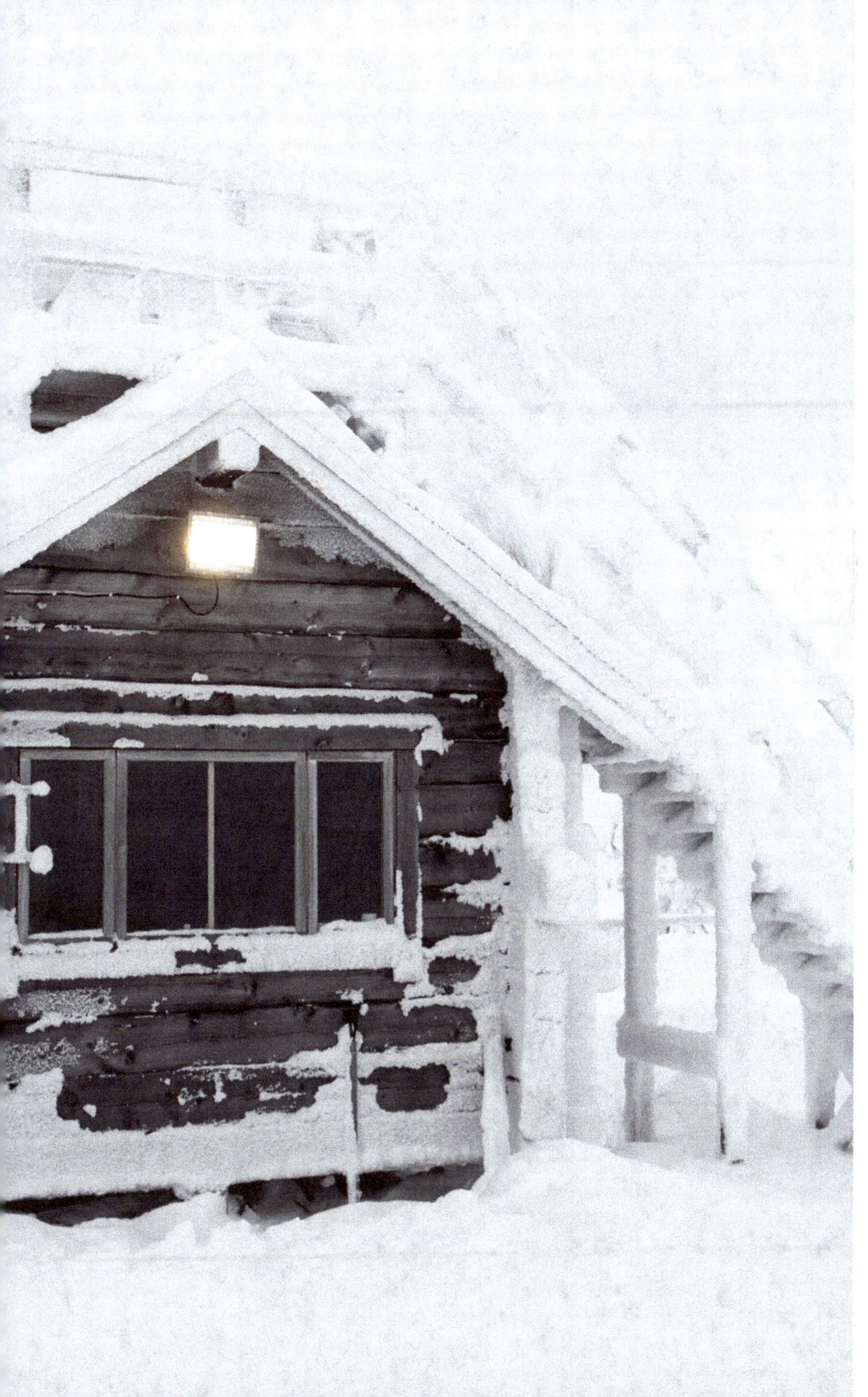

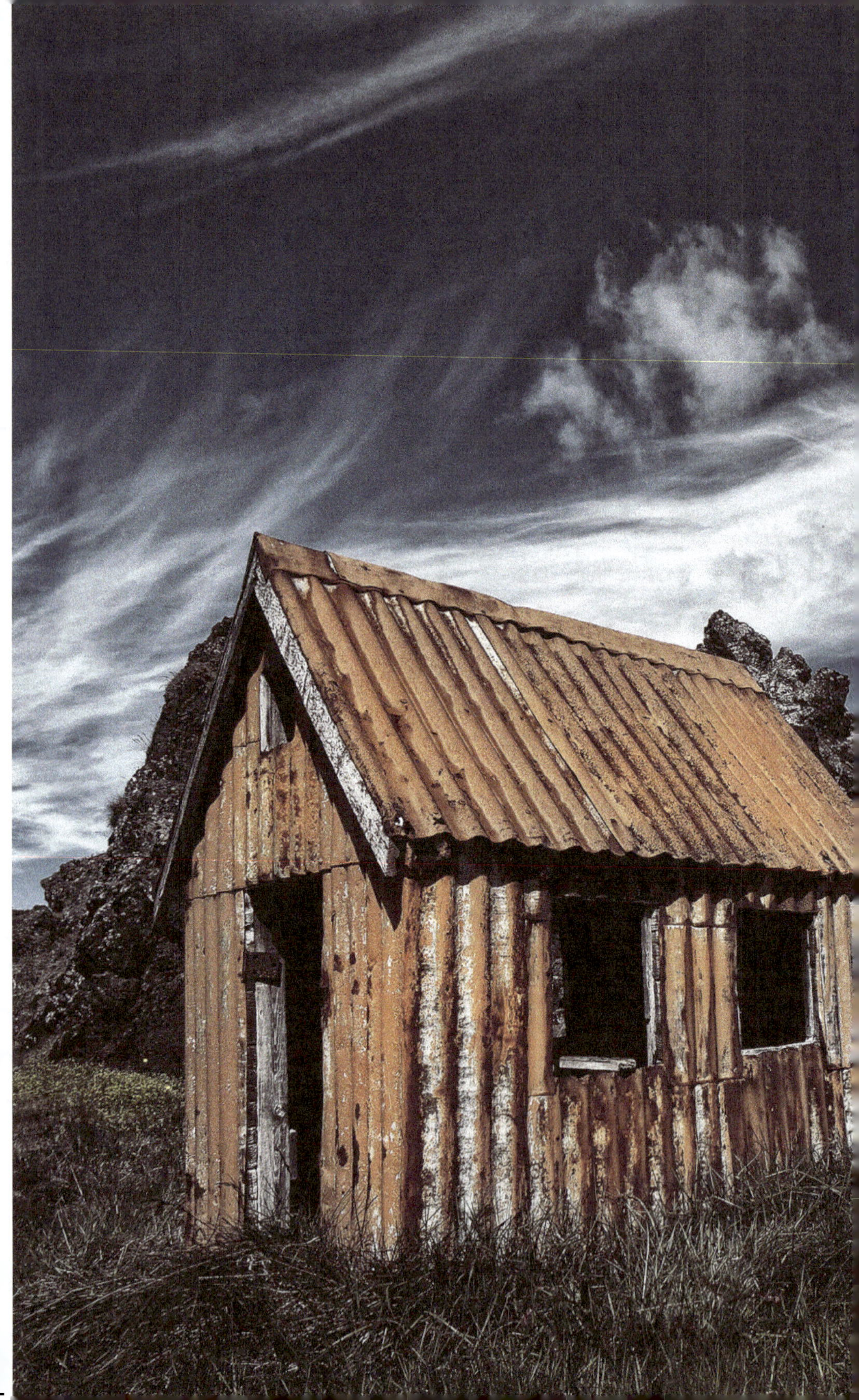

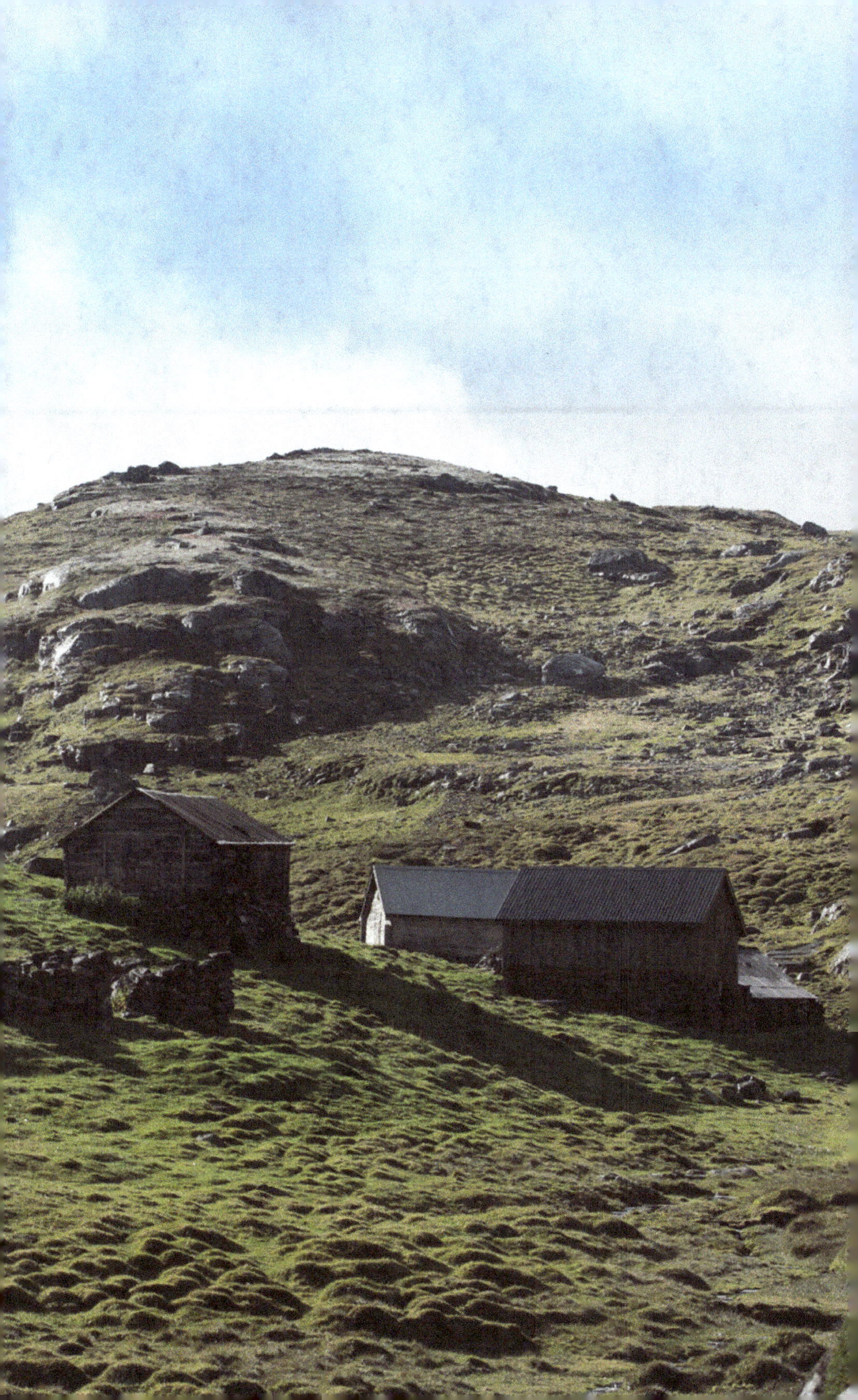

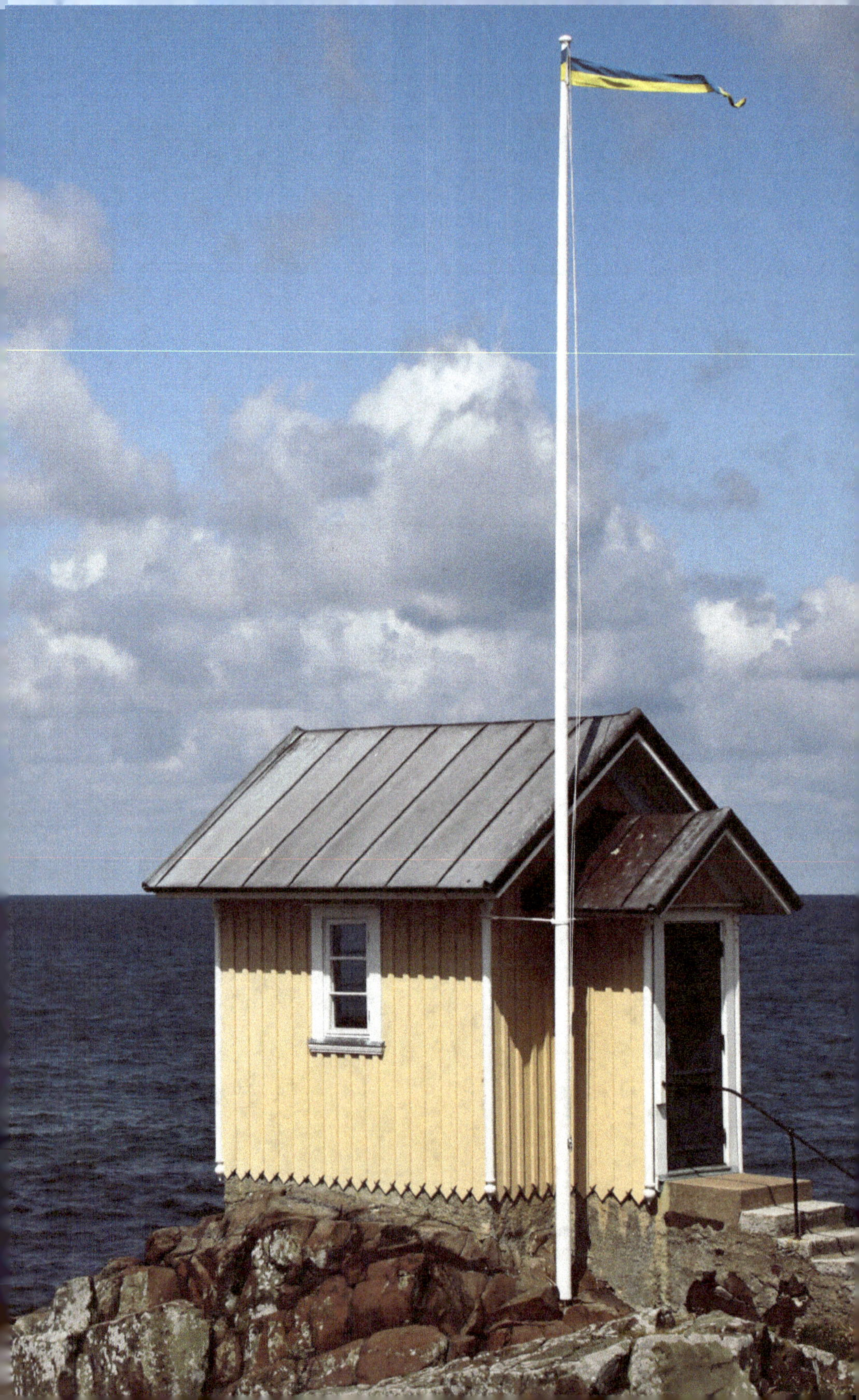

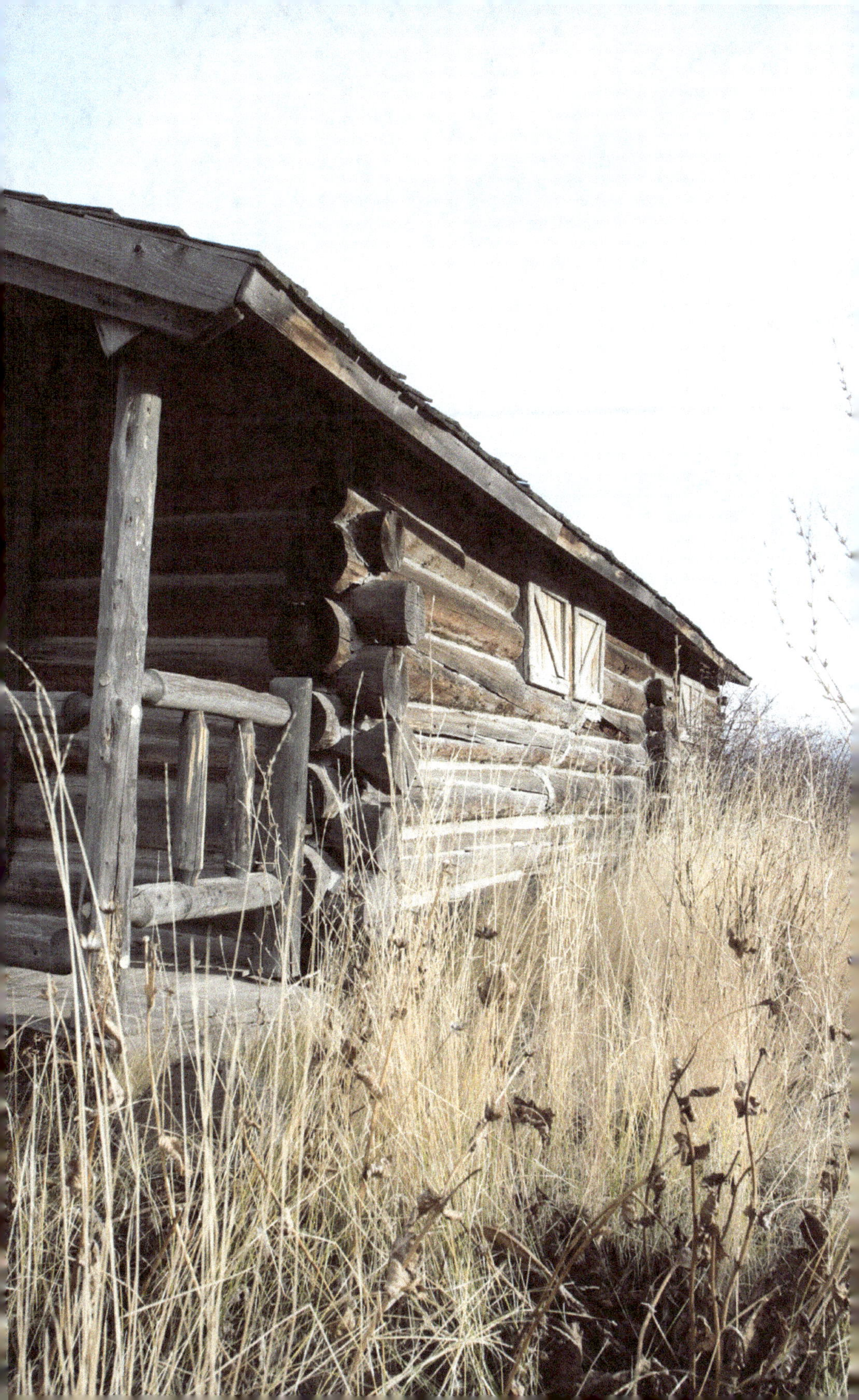

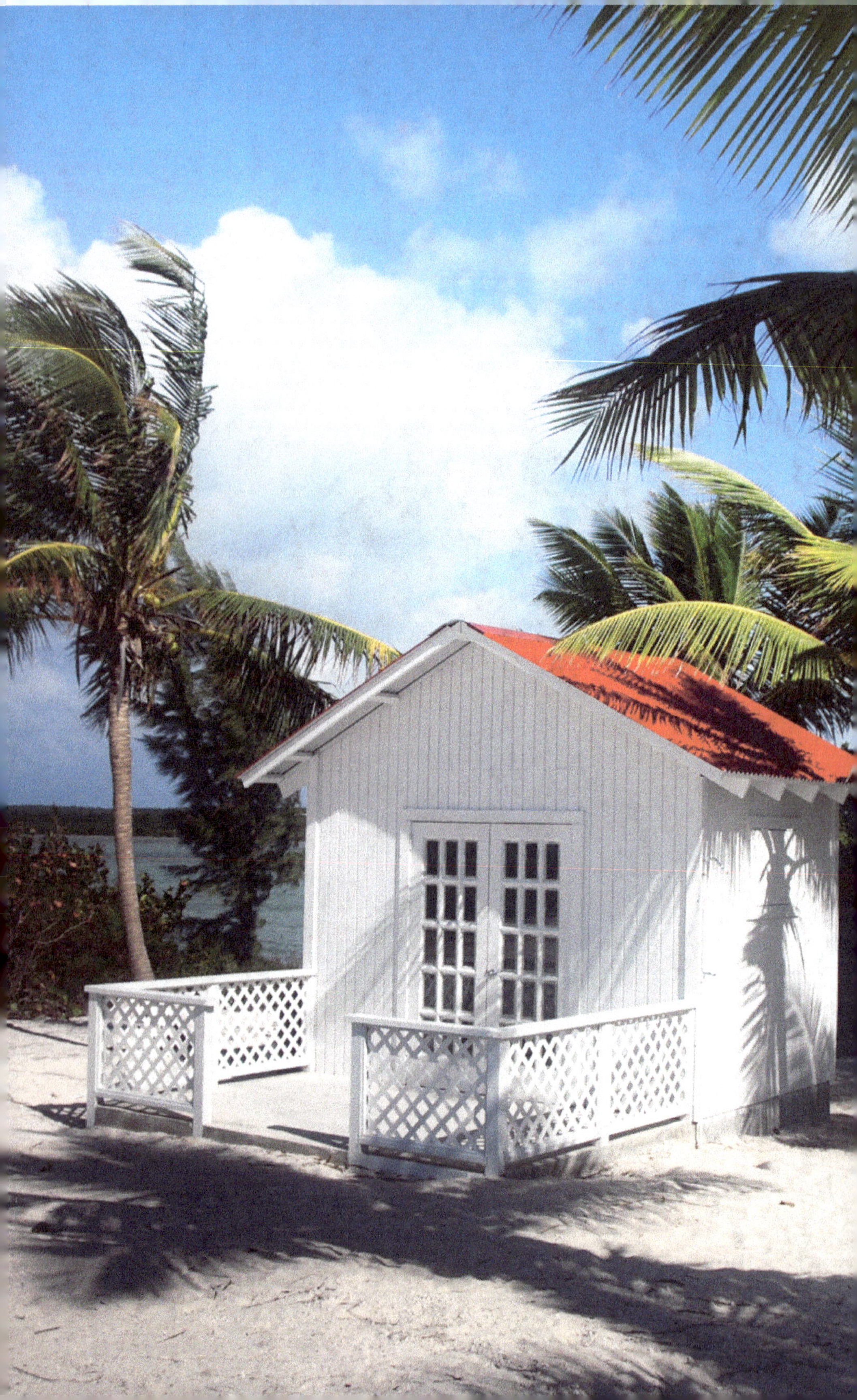

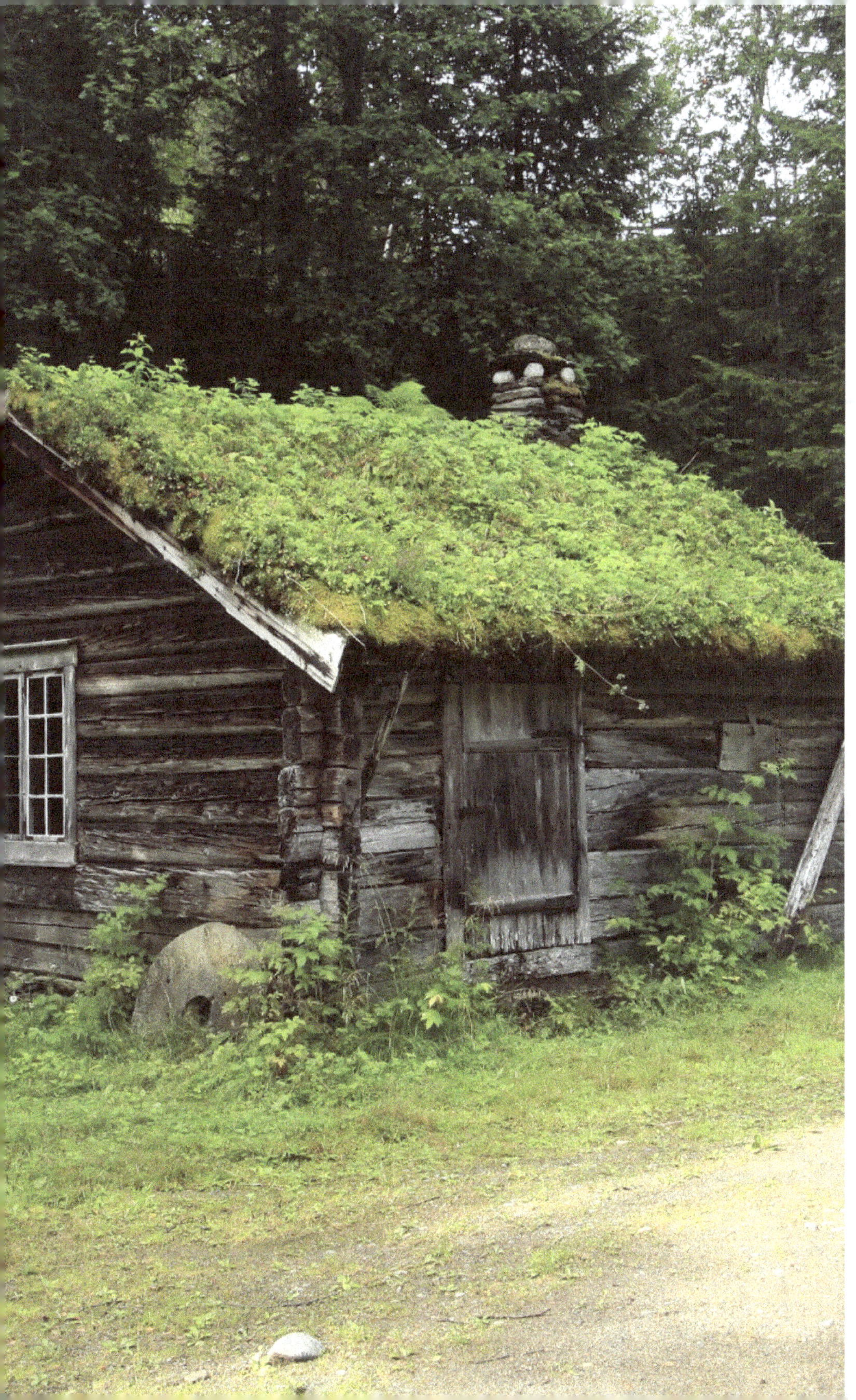

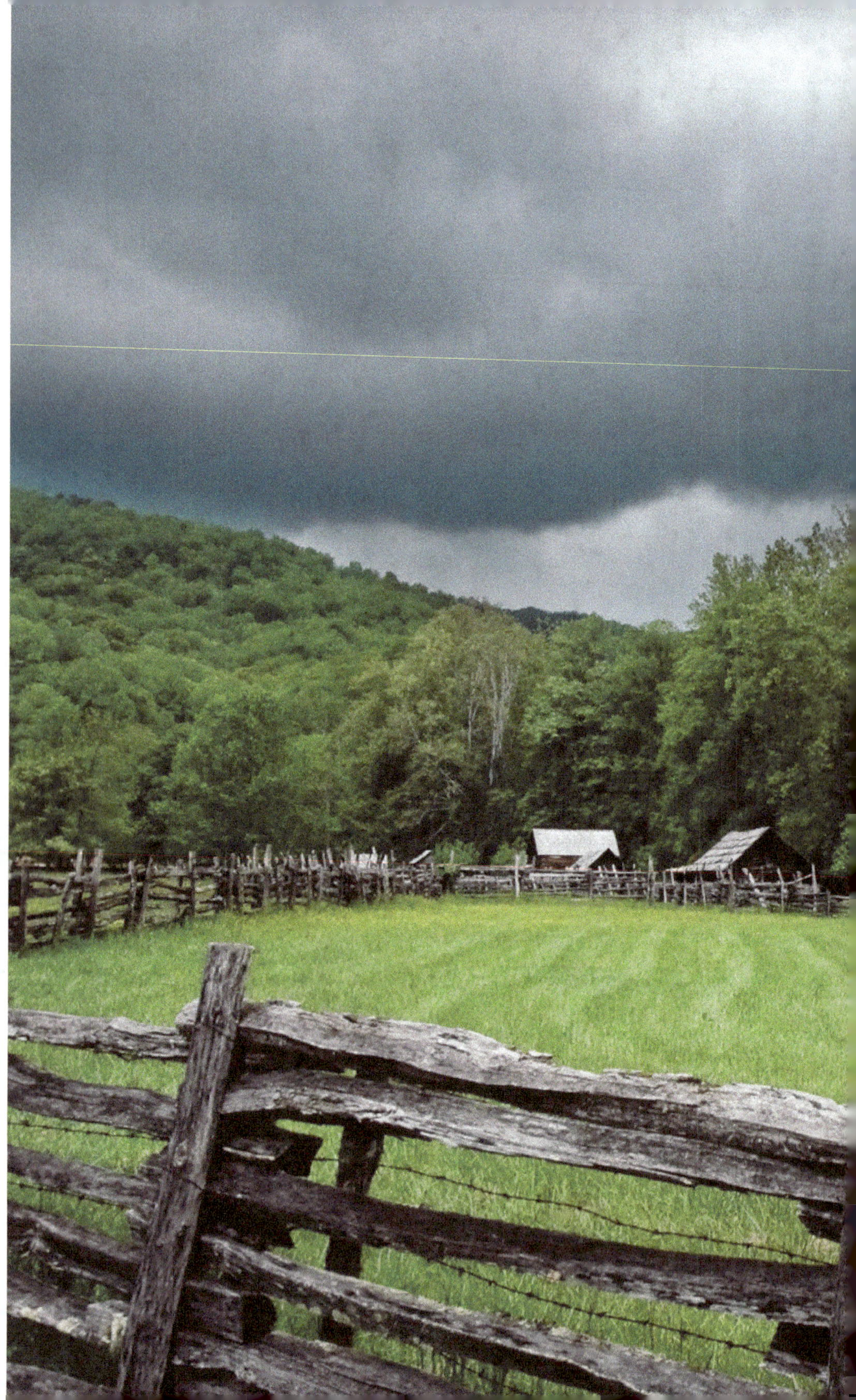

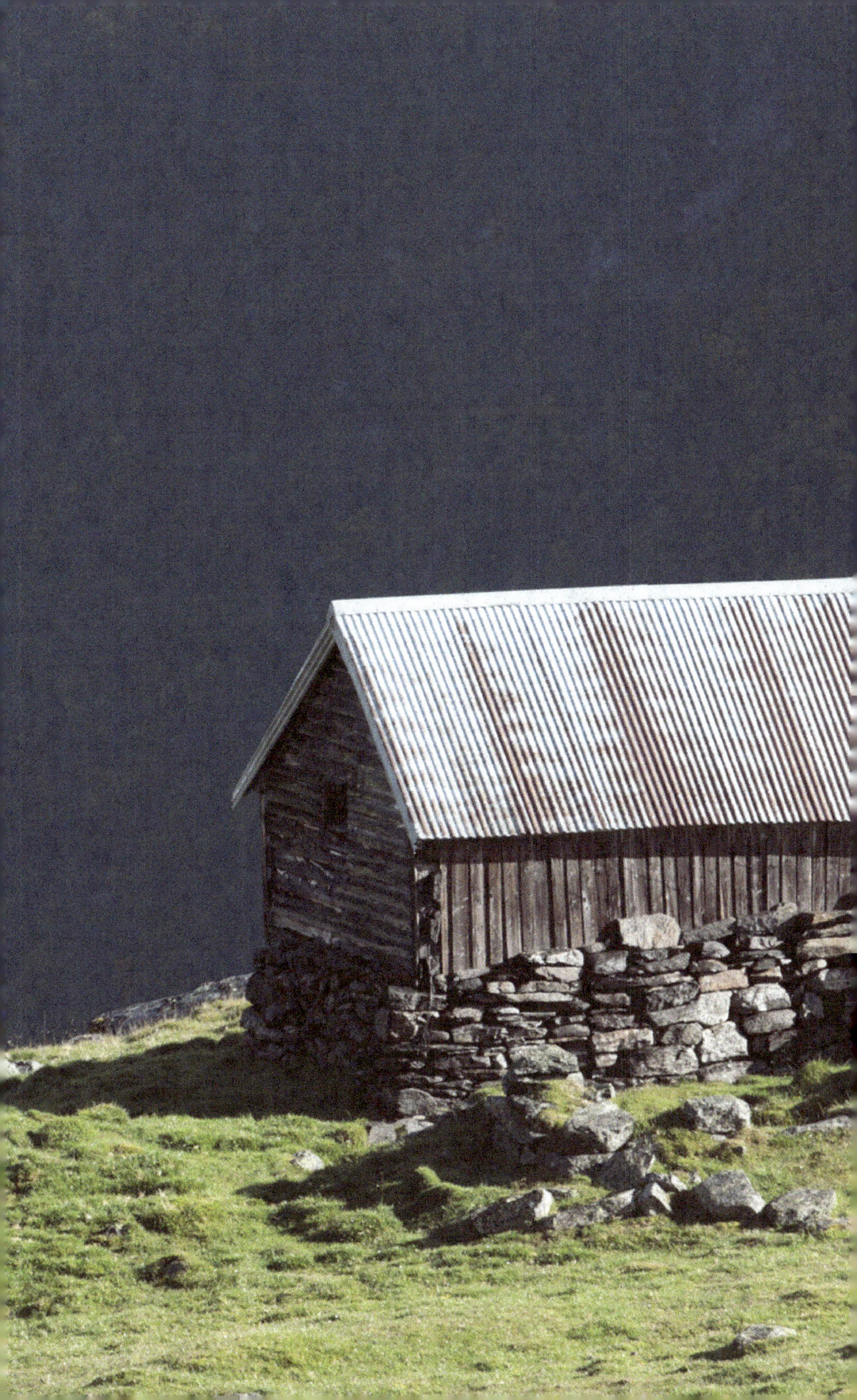

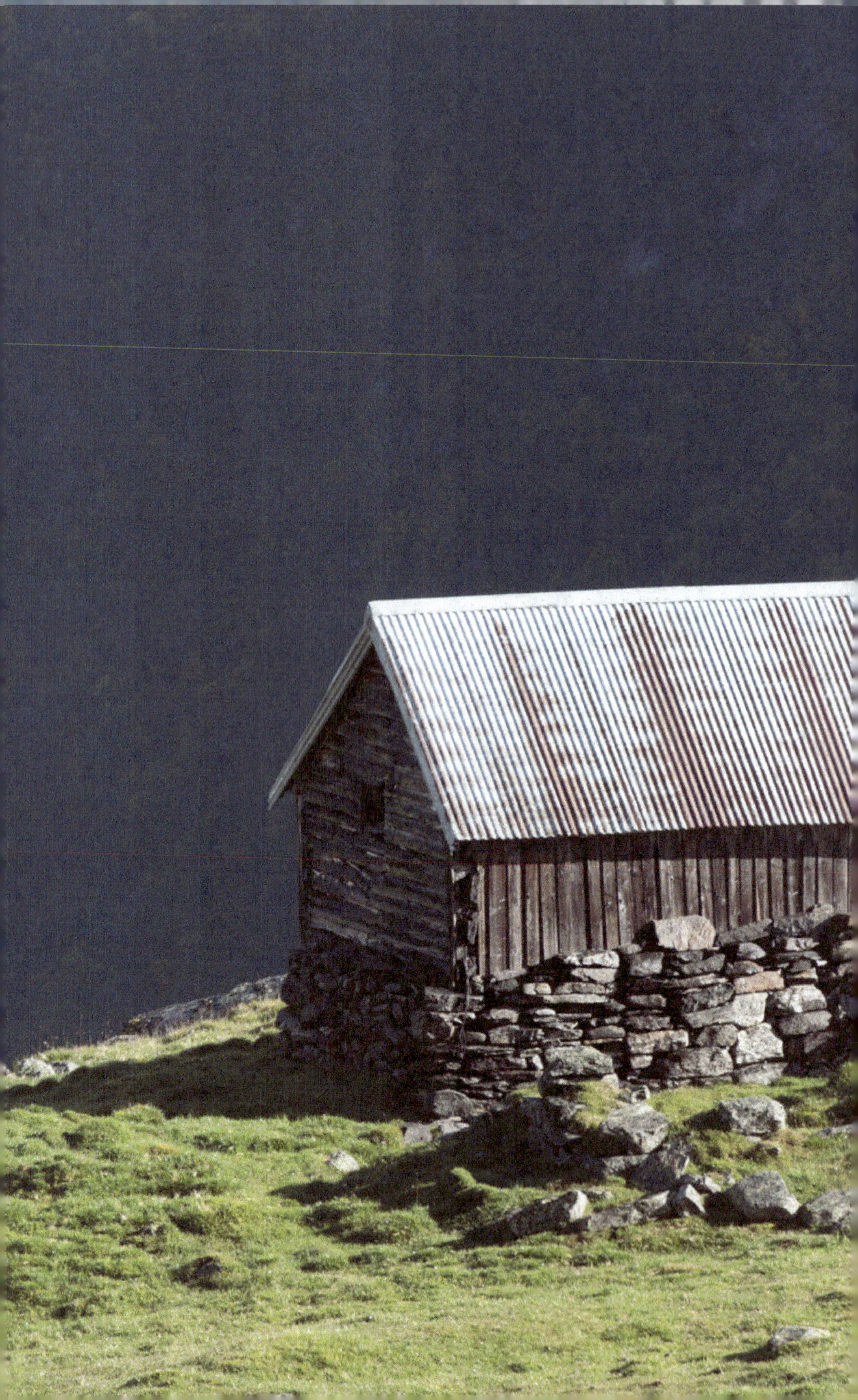

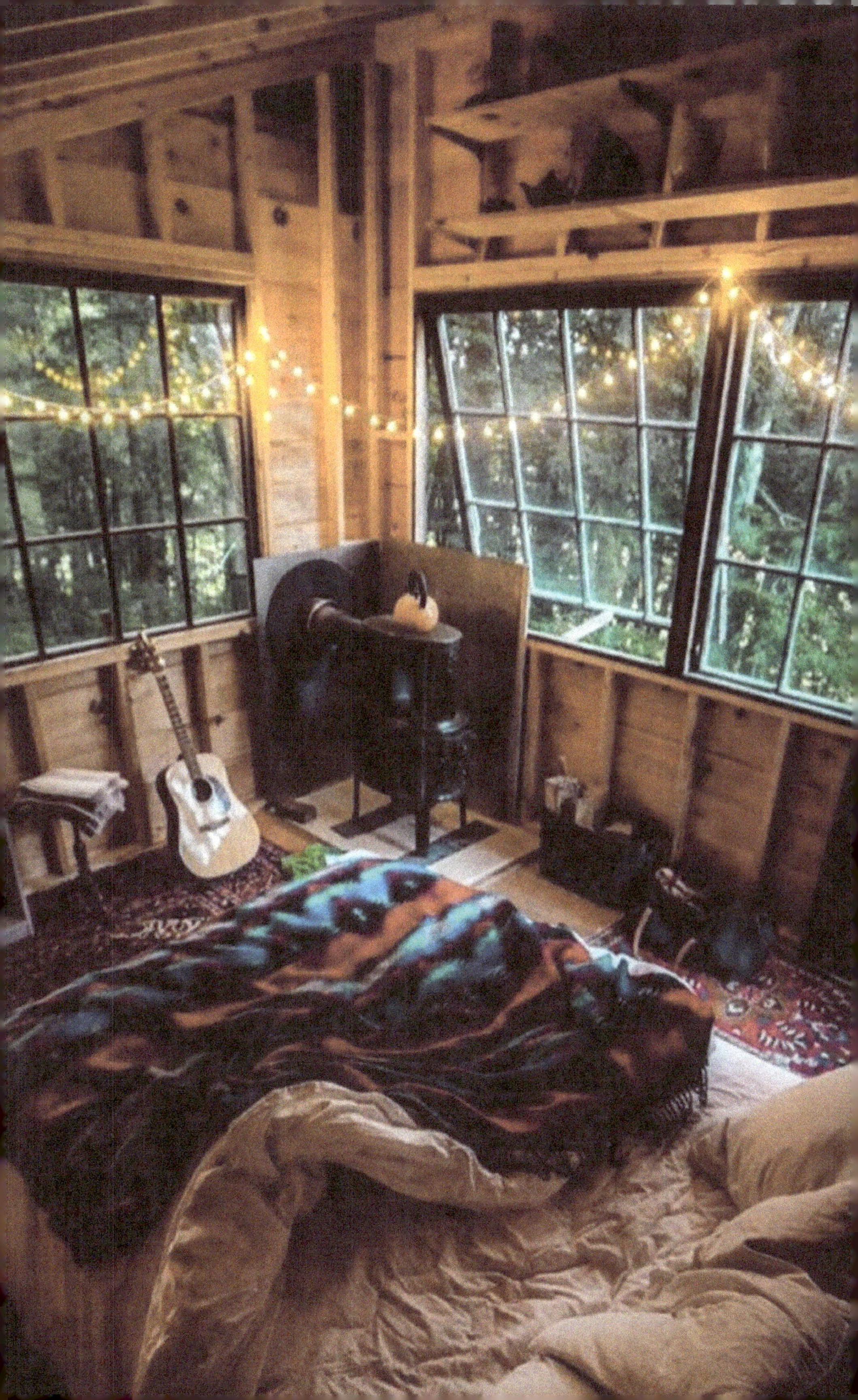

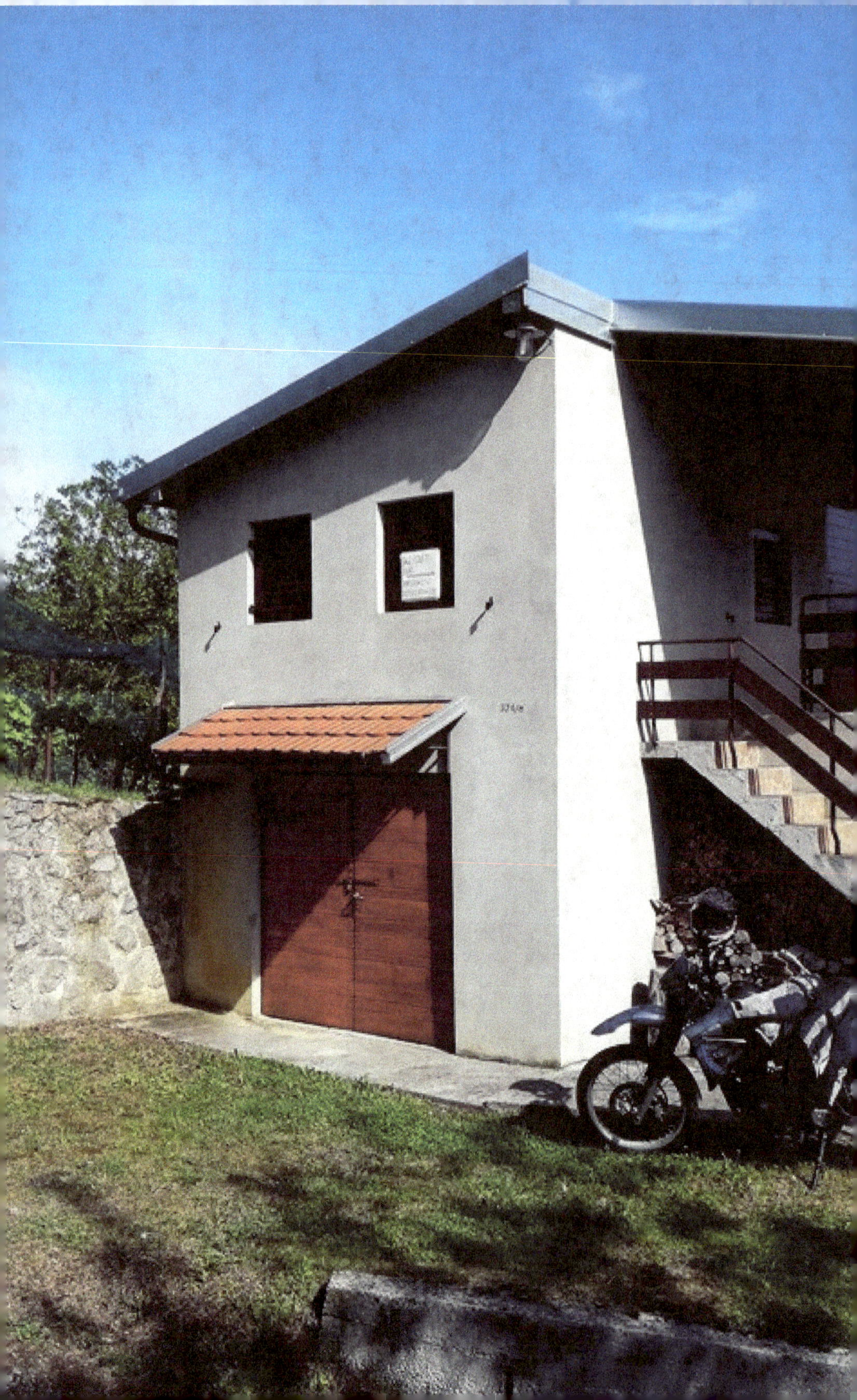

www.ingramcontent.com/pod-product-compliance
Lightning Source LLC
Chambersburg PA
CBHW061723250726
48657CB00002B/738